RADIOACTIVE!

Also by WINIFRED CONKLING

Passenger on the Pearl:
The True Story of Emily Edmonson's Flight from Slavery

RADIOACTIVE!

How Irène Curie
& Lise Meitner
Revolutionized Science
and Changed
the World

WINIFRED CONKLING

ALGONQUIN YOUNG READERS
2016

Published by
Algonquin Young Readers
an imprint of Algonquin Books of Chapel Hill
Post Office Box 2225
Chapel Hill, North Carolina 27515-2225

a division of
Workman Publishing
225 Varick Street
New York, New York 10014

Printed in the United States of America.
Published simultaneously in Canada by Thomas Allen & Son Limited.
Design: Anne Winslow and Steve Godwin. Layout: Jacky Woolsey.

PHOTO CREDITS

Corbis: pages 12, 66, 89, 181, 189; Curie Museum / Musée Curie (Coll. ACJC):
pages 6, 21, 22, 26, 29, 32, 33, 39, 40, 42, 47, 49, 55, 58, 61, 97; Fotolibra:
page 51; Wikipedia Commons: pages 2, 16, 44, 48, 52, 63, 65, 70, 72, 74,
83, 85, 92, 94, 101, 103, 111, 115, 117, 127, 143, 148, 149, 152, 154,
155, 161, 165, 167, 170, 184, 185.

LIBRARY OF CONGRESS CATALOGING-IN-PUBLICATION DATA
Conkling, Winifred, author.
Radioactive! : how Irène Curie and Lise Meitner revolutionized science
and changed the world / by Winifred Conkling.—First edition.
pages cm
Includes bibliographical references and index.
Audience: 12 and up.
Audience: 7–8.
ISBN 978-1-61620-415-0
1. Joliot-Curie, Irène, 1897–1956—Juvenile literature. 2. Women scientists—
France—Biography—Juvenile literature. 3. Meitner, Lise, 1878–1968—Juvenile
literature. 4. Women scientists—Germany—Biography—Juvenile literature.
5. Radioactivity—Juvenile literature. 6. Nuclear fission—Juvenile literature. I. Title.
QC774.J65C66 2016
539.7'52—dc23   2015017256

10 9 8 7 6 5 4 3 2 1
First Edition

CONTENTS

··

A WORD ABOUT NAMES

This is the story of Lise Meitner and Irène Curie, but it also covers events in the lives of other members of the Curie family, including Marie Curie, Pierre Curie, Eve Curie, and Frédéric Joliot-Curie. To make matters more confusing, as a married woman Irène sometimes used the name Curie and other times Joliot-Curie. While it is customary to refer to a subject by last name on second and subsequent references, in the text the Curies are referred to by their first names if there is any possibility of confusion. The use of first names is intended to promote clarity; it is never meant to minimize status or respect.

RADIOACTIVE!

1

"THE MOST BEAUTIFUL EXPERIMENT IN THE WORLD"

THEIR MOMENT HAD finally arrived. In the fall of 1933, scientists Irène and Frédéric Joliot-Curie were invited to present their latest research at the 7th Solvay Conference in Brussels, Belgium. The French researchers were thrilled to have a chance to appear before their intellectual idols, 40 of the best and brightest nuclear physicists in the world, and impress them with their insights into the structure and properties of the atom and how it worked.

The Joliot-Curies were among the youngest scientists at the conference: Irène was 36 years old and Frédéric was 33. As a research team they had earned a reputation for doing interesting work in the past few years, but this promised to be their breakout moment; their chance to step out from the shadow cast by Irène's parents, Nobel Prize–winning scientists Marie and Pierre Curie. Marie had attended this conference every year, but this was the first time that Irène and Frédéric had been invited.

Frédéric almost always came across as poised and confident, but when it was his turn to stand behind the podium he was noticeably nervous. Most of the men in attendance had fashionable mustaches

Forty of the world's leading physicists attended the 7th Solvay Conference in Brussels, Belgium, in October 1933. Irène Joliot-Curie is seated in the front row, second from the left. Lise Meitner is in the front row, second from the right. Marie Curie is seated in the first row, fifth from the left. Frédéric Joliot-Curie is standing in the second row, third from the left.

or beards; Frédéric's clean-shaven face made him appear even younger than he was. Irène stood by Frédéric as he presented their research findings, which suggested a new way of thinking about the architecture of the atom.

Physicists at the turn of the 20th century were just beginning to understand atomic structure. We now know that atoms—the basic building blocks of matter—consist of a core called a nucleus, which is made up of particles called protons (with a positive charge) and neutrons (with no charge), and that the nucleus is circled by electrons (with a negative charge). While this information is considered elementary today, scientists were just figuring it out in the 1930s.

At the time the Joliot-Curies were presenting their research, physicists thought that the nucleus of the atom consisted of protons and electrons, positive and negative particles. In the 1930s, atomic structure was uncharted territory for even the most brilliant physicists. Nobel Prize–winning physicist Wolfgang Pauli explained the

A (VERY) BRIEF HISTORY OF ATOMIC STRUCTURE

- Ancient Greek philosopher **Democritus** (460–370 BC) proposed the theory that everything in the universe is made up of tiny, indivisible, indestructible particles known as atoms.

- **John Dalton** (1766–1844) suggested that atoms could combine to form compounds. He envisioned atoms as solid spheres.

- **Joseph John Thomson** (1856–1940) discovered negatively charged electrons. He developed the "plum pudding model" of the atom in which a large, positively charged mass (the plum pudding) contains a number of randomly dispersed negatively charged small electrons (the raisins in the pudding). A more modern model would be chocolate chips in a cookie or blueberries in a muffin.

- **Ernest Rutherford** (1871–1937) changed the understanding of atomic structure in 1911. He conducted an experiment in which he fired electrons through a sheet of gold foil. Most of the electrons passed straight through, but a few were deflected, or knocked out of alignment. From that, Rutherford determined that most of the mass of a gold atom was concentrated in a central nucleus which was surrounded by electrons.

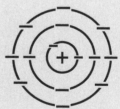

- **Niels Bohr** (1885–1962) argued that electrons revolved around the nucleus in fixed orbits, much like planets rotating around the sun. His model included a nucleus made up of protons and neutrons.

- The **modern model**, sometimes called the **electron cloud model**, refines Bohr's model by acknowledging that it's impossible to know the exact position or speed of an electron at any one moment. Instead of fixed electron shells, this model shows electrons as inhabiting a cloud, which indicates the probable position of an electron rather than a firm boundary. This model takes into account the complex and erratic behavior of electrons.

state of knowledge when he said, "Physics is once again very fouled up, and for me it is so difficult that I wish I were a film comedian or something like that and had never heard of physics in the first place."

The research that Irène and Frédéric presented at the Solvay Conference challenged what was believed about atomic structure at that time. When the Joliot-Curies presented their findings about neutrons, the scientists in the room were not convinced. Instead of giving the praise Irène and Frédéric had hoped for, their colleagues questioned their results. British physicist Patrick Blackett challenged the Joliot-Curies' interpretation of their research. As Irène took the floor and tried to defend their findings, the audience whispered to one another and remained dubious.

Then Lise Meitner, a German scientist with an impeccable reputation, raised her hand.

The room quieted. The chairman called on her, and Meitner stood and said: "My colleagues and I have done similar experiments. We have been unable to uncover a *single* neutron." She then sat down.

Everyone in the crowd turned toward Irène and Frédéric, waiting for a response. Meitner was known for her meticulous work and brilliant experimental design. Irène and Frédéric were fairly new to the field, and no one was quite sure what to think about them yet. In recent years, the French duo had come close to making several important discoveries, but they had also made critical mistakes in the interpretation of their results. Had that happened again?

There was silence followed by chaos as everyone in the room began arguing at once. Irène and Frédéric stood in front of the crowd and stared at each other, embarrassed and confused.

The conference director announced a break to give everyone a chance to stretch their legs and calm down. Marie Curie had attended the conference, but she was caught in a conversation, so Irène and Frédéric walked back into the gardens alone, still baffled and a little angry about what had happened. They did not object to having their hypothesis tested in follow-up experiments, but they did not expect the accuracy of their findings to be challenged in public.

Irène and Frédéric felt confident that they had not made a mistake in their research—not this time. They had checked and rechecked their results. They had considered every possible explanation of their results. They did not want to miss out on credit for this important scientific breakthrough.

During the break, most of the other delegates at the conference huddled together in small groups, but did not include Irène and Frédéric in their conversations. The message was clear: The intellectual elite sided with Meitner and assumed that the Joliot-Curies had made another mistake. Perhaps the young French couple had been working too fast, trying too hard to make a discovery before someone else stepped in and did it first.

Only two of their colleagues offered any words of encouragement. The Danish physicist Niels Bohr approached them during the break and said, "What you are doing is of the greatest importance." Later, Austrian Wolfgang Pauli told them, "Congratulations. Don't give up." Perhaps these men realized that, if Irène and Frédéric were correct, then the nucleus of the atom was much more complex than researchers currently believed it to be. They certainly knew that physics still held mysteries and that there was a great deal they did not yet understand.

The Night Everything Clicked

Irène and Frédéric returned to their laboratories at the Radium Institute in Paris downhearted but determined to restore their reputations. Irène believed in their research, and although she did not challenge Lise Meitner at the conference, Irène did intend to repeat her experiments and defend her findings.

What seemed at first to be a setback proved to be an advantage: Because the Joliot-Curies' work had been so widely dismissed, none of the other researchers was interested in investigating their claims or repeating their experiments. For Irène and Frédéric, that meant that they had no competition with their research. The Joliet-Curies repeated their experiments and got the same results. They continued their work, making small changes to their approach.

On January 11, 1934, three months after the conference, Irène and Frédéric worked late into the evening. Irène spent her time in a chemistry lab upstairs, while Frédéric did his experiments in the physics lab in the basement. Frédéric used his favorite research instrument, the Wilson cloud chamber, which was named for its inventor, Scottish physicist Charles Wilson. The device allowed scientists to observe things they could not see with the naked eye. Frédéric had made some modifications to the device, but the basic operation was unchanged: It consisted of a glass chamber full of air that had

Irène and Frédéric Joliot-Curie in 1934, a year after they presented their research at the Solvay Conference.

DETAILS OF THE JOLIOT-CURIES' EXPERIMENT PRESENTED AT THE SOLVAY CONFERENCE

In 1932, Irène and Frédéric Joliot-Curie began a series of experiments looking for positrons, a newly discovered type of subatomic particle with the mass of an electron, but a positive instead of a negative charge. In their research, they bombarded different elements with alpha particles, a type of subatomic particle emitted by radioactive elements. When they fired alpha particles at medium-weight elements, they found those elements ejected protons. When they tested lightweight elements, those elements shot out both neutrons and positrons.

The Joliot-Curies wondered why the alpha particles would force out protons in some cases, but both neutrons and positrons in others. Based on their results, they theorized that protons were made up of neutrons and positrons. This was the research that they presented at the Solvay Conference in 1933. (They later learned that their findings were accurate, but that their explanation was not.)

been saturated with water or alcohol vapor. When a particle moved through the chamber, a tiny cloud formed around it and it turned into a water droplet. As it moved through the chamber, the particle would leave a misty trail, making its path, or vapor trail, visible.

By watching the vapor trails in the cloud chamber, researchers could see the movement of the subatomic particles. The vapor tracks—like the contrails of airplanes in flight—only lasted a fraction of a second, so a high-speed camera was attached to the Wilson cloud chamber to photograph the droplets so their movements could be analyzed later. "An infinitely tiny particle projected in this enclosed region can trace its own path, thanks to the succession of drops of condensation," Frédéric said. "Isn't it the most beautiful experiment in the world?"

In addition to the Wilson cloud chamber, the Joliot-Curies used radioactive elements in their research. Unlike the atoms of stable elements, which do not release energy, the atoms of radioactive elements are always decaying, or breaking down into subatomic particles and giving off energy. By placing a sample of radioactive polonium near the Wilson cloud chamber, the Joliot-Curies could see the alpha particles that were released by the polonium. By putting stable elements between the radioactive source and the Wilson cloud chamber, they could determine if the alpha particles were blocked by the stable element, if they changed as they passed through the stable element, or if the alpha particle caused the release of a different subatomic particle, such as a neutron or a proton.

Frédéric set out to perform a new experiment with a Wilson cloud chamber and a Geiger counter, a device that measures radioactivity. In their original experiment, the Joliot-Curies placed a sheet of aluminum foil between the polonium and the Wilson cloud chamber. They wondered if the speed with which the particles hit the aluminum might have an impact on the types of particles that were released, which could explain why other researchers might not have obtained the same results that they did.

In this follow-up experiment, Frédéric placed the polonium next to the aluminum and used the Wilson cloud chamber to measure the particles that passed through, just as he and Irène had done in their original experiment. This time though, he slowly moved the polonium away from the aluminum with the Geiger counter still on. He expected the speed of the rays from the polonium to grow weaker as the distance between the two elements increased, but he found something much more interesting.

To his astonishment, the Geiger counter's *click-click-click*, which reflected the presence of radioactivity, continued even when the

ALPHA, BETA, AND GAMMA RAYS

At the turn of the 20th century, scientists discovered three types of radiation, which they named alpha, beta, and gamma after the first three letters of the Greek alphabet. We now know that an unstable radioactive nucleus tries to become stable by releasing one of three types of radiation:

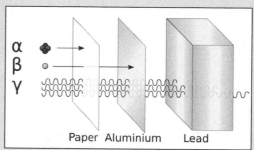

- **Alpha (α) Radiation**: An alpha particle is a helium nucleus (two protons and two neutrons). They are relatively large, heavy particles. They can only travel a few inches through air before being stopped, and they cannot penetrate human skin or clothing. A piece of paper is dense enough to block them. However, alpha particles can be dangerous if ingested or inhaled in the form of radon gas.

- **Beta (β) Radiation**: A beta particle is an electron ejected by a radioactive element. They can travel about six inches through the air before being stopped. Beta particles can penetrate human skin to the layer where new cells are formed. Heavy clothing provides some protection; a one-inch-thick piece of wood or a sheet of aluminum foil can shield most beta radiation.

  Beta decay can happen in one of two ways: either a proton breaks down into a neutron and a positive charge, or a neutron breaks down into a proton and a negative charge.

- **Gamma (γ) Radiation**: A gamma ray is a short-wavelength, high-energy packet of electromagnetic radiation. Unlike alpha and beta radiation, which are made of subatomic particles, gamma radiation takes the form of pure energy, so it is referred to as a "ray" rather than a "particle."

  Gamma rays can travel from hundreds to thousands of feet through the air, and can deeply penetrate and harm human tissue. Dense materials are needed to shield gamma radiation, such as several inches of lead or several feet of concrete.

polonium was held at a distance. Frédéric had expected the sound from the Geiger counter to fade to silence, but the clatter continued for several minutes. He didn't know how, but the aluminum was acting as if it had become radioactive.

Frédéric didn't trust himself. The result didn't make sense. He repeated the experiment and heard the telltale clicking again. Had something happened to make the aluminum radioactive?

Frédéric bounded up the stairs, taking them two at a time, hurrying to reach Irène's lab. He brought her back downstairs to watch the experiment without telling her what to expect. He repeated the test and again heard the sound of the Geiger counter let out its frantic clicking, gradually calming and going quiet after several minutes. Irène immediately understood the significance of the clattering Geiger counter: radioactivity. The polonium had transferred its radioactivity to the aluminum. *They had created artificial radioactivity.* This was a life-changing discovery, the career-defining breakthrough that Irène and Frédéric had been had been working for.

Proving Themselves

Irène and Frédéric knew what they had to do: They had three days to prepare a detailed report for the French Academy of Science's regular Monday meeting. They spent Friday and Saturday working on the project. At about 7 PM on Saturday, one of their colleagues was leaving the laboratory for the evening. Frédéric called him in and asked him to repeat the experiment without explaining any of the details. At that point, the Joliot-Curies needed a third party to independently confirm their findings. Their coworker repeated their experiment and achieved the same results.

The Joliot-Curies had created a short-lived radioactive element. Alpha particles—which are made of two protons and two neutrons bound together—are a type of radiation released during radioactive decay. The Joliot-Curies understood that during their experiment

CREATING ARTIFICIAL RADIOACTIVITY

The Joliot-Curies' experiment demonstrates the process of *transmutation,* or one chemical element being transformed or changed into another. In this case, the aluminum is changed into radioactive phosphorus and then into silicon.

aluminum + alpha particles → artificially radioactive phosphorus + neutron

The artificially radioactive phosphorous has a half life of 3 1/2 minutes, so it decays after that time into silicon:

Artificially radioactive phosphorus → Silicon + Beta radiation

the aluminum had absorbed alpha particles from the polonium and—for a period of about three and a half minutes—transformed into an artificially radioactive form of phosphorus before decaying into another more stable element, silicon. The phosphorus was radioactive and unstable; the silicon was nonradioactive and stable. They knew that their claim would be unbelievable, so they needed physical and visual proof of their claim before they could announce it to the world.

The short half-life meant that Irène and Frédéric had only a few minutes to work and collect the data they needed during the course of the experiment. Before they started, they laid out all of the equipment they needed and practiced the procedure to ensure that they worked accurately and efficiently. This was their chance to prove themselves and they did not intend to have any errors in their research.

Irène had come up with an ingenious test design, one which demanded that she and Frédéric work quickly and accurately. First,

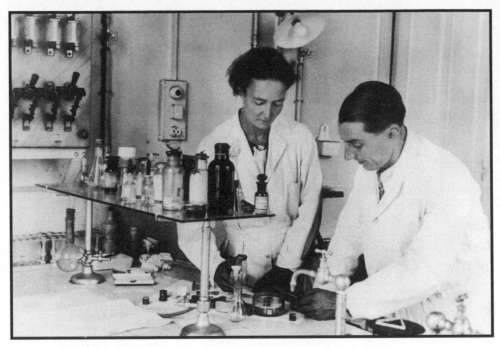

Irène and Frédéric Joliot-Curie at work in a lab at the Radium Institute in Paris, France.

Frédéric placed the aluminum near the polonium, creating a newly radioactive form of aluminum. He then put the radioactive aluminum in a vial with a stopper on top. Next, Irène added hydrochloric acid to the vial. As the acid dissolved the metal, the chemical reaction between the acid and metal produced hydrogen and radioactive phosphorus gases. Irène removed the radioactive gas from the vial, leaving inert (non-radioactive) aluminum salts behind. The Geiger counter confirmed that the gas itself was radioactive, and another follow-up test proved that the gas was indeed phosphorus. When the experiment worked, Irène watched with pleasure as Frédéric jumped up and down throughout the basement of the Radium Institute. The discovery was of major importance—not only for themselves as scientists, but for the world.

At the turn of the 20th century, Marie and Pierre Curie's

discovery of *natural* radioactivity had revolutionized science and laid the foundation for the study of atomic physics. Using radioactive elements, researchers were able to conduct experiments that allowed them to develop and test theories about atomic structure that fundamentally changed their understanding of how the world worked.

Now, Irène and Frédéric Joliot-Curie's discovery of *artificial* radioactivity was poised to change the world of physics again. Natural radioactive elements were scarce and expensive. The creation of artificial radioactive elements meant that they could be manufactured in a lab, making them much more accessible and affordable.

Discovering artificial radioactivity was the first step in a nuclear science revolution. Frédéric later said, "Scientists, building up or shattering elements at will, will be able to bring about transmutations of an explosive type." While Frédéric may have imagined the exciting possibilities ahead for scientists who could change one element into another, he did not predict that artificial radioactivity would ultimately lead to the discovery of nuclear fission and the creation of the most powerful and deadly weapon known to humanity: the atomic bomb.

The Demonstration

Later that weekend, Irène and Frédéric invited Marie Curie and Paul Langevin, Frédéric's mentor and a close family friend, into the lab to witness the experiment. The entire process took about half an hour. Frédéric later recalled the moment he and Irène shared their discovery with Marie, whose fingertips had been scarred and burned by years of handling radium and other radioactive elements in her own work:

> I will never forget the expression of intense joy, which overtook her when Irène and I showed her the first [artificially produced] radioactive element in a little glass tube.

I can see her still taking this little tube of the radioelement, already quite weak, in her radium-damaged fingers. To verify what we were telling her, she brought the Geiger-Müller counter up close to it and she could hear the numerous clicks. . . . This was without a doubt the last great satisfaction of her life.

Irène and Frédéric presented their historic report, "A New Type of Radioactivity," to the French Academy that Monday, just four days after Frédéric's initial observation. Their report in *Les Comptes Rendus de l'Académie des Sciences* presented the evidence that they had created artificial radioactivity. They followed that report with a letter to the journal *Nature* a few days later.

British physicist Ernest Rutherford wrote to congratulate the Joliot-Curies on their success, noting that he had tried similar experiments without success. Considering the catastrophe of the Solvay Conference, Irène and Frédéric were overjoyed to be proven correct. They had been right; Lise Meitner had been wrong. In the experiment they presented at the Solvay Conference, the Joliot-Curies *had* found both protons and a combination of neutrons and positrons. What they had not understood then—nor had anyone else at the conference—was that their experiment had triggered a two-step process: When exposed to the alpha particles from the polonium, the aluminum released a neutron and became radioactive; then, several minutes later, in a second nuclear reaction, the radioactive aluminum released a positron and changed to stable silicon. Their data had been accurate, and now they could explain why.

Meitner later sent a letter to congratulate Irène and Frédéric on their work. She wrote: "The significance of these extraordinarily beautiful results is certainly very far-reaching." Their paper on artificial radioactivity not only restored their reputations as leading researchers, but its importance put them on the shortlist as candidates for the Nobel Prize in physics.

Irène took personal pride in having created the first manmade radioactive element and being able to share the experience with her aging mother. In that moment, the scientific work and passion of two generations of the Curie family merged: Marie and Pierre Curie had discovered natural radioactivity, and their daughter and son-in-law had discovered artificial radioactivity. This proved to be one of the greatest and last moments of joy in Marie Curie's life.

In the months that followed their discovery of artificial radio-activity, Irène watched her mother's health decline. By the summer of 1934, Marie Curie no longer had the strength to visit the Radium Institute. She was frail and feeble, and she suffered from a lingering fever. A specialist from Geneva assessed Marie's condition and diagnosed her with aplastic pernicious anemia, a disease of the bone marrow, with no hope of recovery. The disease was caused by exposure to high levels of radiation.

Irène was a strong and stoic woman, but she was so distraught at the thought of her mother's death that she could not bear to stay with Marie for long periods of time. Instead, Irène's younger sister, Eve, sat by her mother's bedside. Marie Curie died on July 4, 1934. On that day, Irène lost not only her mother, but her mentor and role model.

THE DISCOVERY OF NATURAL RADIOACTIVITY

Irène and Frédéric Joliot-Curie's discovery of artificial radioactivity was a groundbreaking advancement in the world of physics. The study of naturally occurring radioactivity had begun almost 40 years before, in 1895, when German physicist Wilhelm Röntgen discovered that a luminous green glow appeared when high-voltage electric currents were passed through certain gases at low pressure. His experiment produced an "invisible light" that could pass through wood and books and human flesh, although it could not penetrate metal or denser materials. When Röntgen placed his hand in front of a screen filled with this special gas, he could see the shadows of his bones. He called the strange rays *X-rays* because he wasn't sure what they were. (He assumed he'd give them a more appropriate name later, but the term caught on.)

French physicist Antoine Henri Becquerel became interested in the phenomenon. Becquerel specialized in fluorescence and phosphorescence — things that glow in the dark when exposed to light or after having been exposed to light — and he wanted to know whether materials that exhibited these qualities might be the source of these so-called X-rays. He tested various stones and wood from his collections, but none produced X-rays. He moved on to various

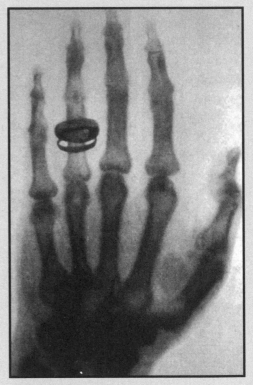

Wilhelm Röntgen demonstrated his new X-ray technology at a public lecture in 1896. When his wife saw the image she said, "I have seen my death."

phosphorescent and fluorescent substances, examining each to see if it produced these invisible rays.

To test an object's ability to emit X-rays, Becquerel placed the materials on photographic plates that had been wrapped in thick black paper to test whether the rays could penetrate the paper and create an image. Nothing happened until he tested uranium salts, which did emit radioactive rays.

X-rays were little more than a curiosity until Marie Curie learned about Becquerel's work and decided to study it for her doctoral thesis beginning in 1897.

As part of her investigation, Marie searched for other elements that might also release X-rays; she examined hundreds of metals, salts, oxides, and ores that she had borrowed from the French Museum of Natural History. She found that the mysterious rays were emitted by thorium and pitch-blende, a useless byproduct of mining uranium, copper, and cobalt. Huge piles of pitchblende were in mines in central Europe, where the minerals were used to color pottery and glass.

Working with a sample of pitchblende, Marie isolated the uranium, which she knew to be radioactive. She was surprised to find that a piece of pitchblende was almost four times more radioactive than the pure uranium extracted from it, meaning that another, more radioactive, element must also be present. Marie set out to isolate this unknown, highly radioactive element from the pitchblende.

Intrigued with Marie's research, Pierre joined his wife in the lab. To-gether, the Curies developed a multi-step chemical process to isolate the radioactive ingredients in pitchblende. After each step, they kept the radio-active part and threw away the waste, getting incrementally closer to a puri-fied form of the mysterious new element.

On July 18, 1898, Marie went to a nearby laboratory to ask a colleague to identify the element using a spectrograph. An electric current was run through the element and created a rainbow-like spectrum of color. Since no two elements have the same spectrum, he was able to tell Marie that she had discovered a previously unknown radioactive element. She named it *polonium* in honor of her beloved homeland, Poland.

Five months later, the Curies published a report discussing the probable existence of a second new element, one even more radioactive than the polonium. They named this highly radioactive new element *radium*, from the Latin word for "ray." It took almost four years of steady work, 400 tons of water, and 40 tons of corrosive chemicals to isolate one-tenth of a gram of radioactive material. On March 28, 1902, the Curies finally had enough radium to confirm that they had discovered a highly radioactive new element, one that was one million times more radioactive than uranium.

At the dawn of the 20th century, Marie and Pierre's work on radioactivity had suggested that the atom itself was more complex than scientists had previously assumed. Before the discovery of X-rays and radioactivity, few scientists had much interest in studying atoms because they could not be "seen." Radioactivity provided researchers with new tools to explore the secrets of atomic structure by studying the way elements change and respond when exposed to radiation. Although the Curies did not realize it at the time, the discovery of radium and radioactivity was about to unlock and open the door to modern physics.

UNDERSTANDING RADIOACTIVITY

Radioactive elements are unstable atoms that constantly give off energy in an attempt to reach a state of balance, or equilibrium. Given enough time, all radioactive elements will decay into more stable elements. Some radioactive elements decay in as little as a fraction of a second while others can take billions of years. For example, polonium-215 has a half-life of 0.00178 seconds, while uranium-238 has a half-life of 4.5 billion years.

Before Marie Curie began to study radioactive elements, scientists believed that atoms—the basic building blocks of matter—were impossible to divide or alter. In other words, they thought that an atom of one element could never change into another. The discovery of radioactivity demonstrated that atoms can change, and that radioactive atoms release energy in the process. This insight opened up new questions about the structure of the atom. It became nothing less than the basis of modern chemistry and physics.

In her experiments, Marie learned that the radiation being released from the elements she studied was not affected by chemical process or external conditions, so she concluded that the mysterious rays were an atomic property of the elements that produced them. This discovery was revolutionary: Radioactivity was the first new property of matter discovered since Sir Isaac Newton defined the law of gravity in 1686.

2

LITTLE QUEEN
AND THE OTHER BABY

IRÈNE JOLIOT-CURIE SEEMED destined for a career in science. She was the first-born daughter of two Nobel Prize–winning physicists, and she shared her parents' intellect and their passion for studying the physical world. Irène idolized her mother and used their shared interest in physics as a way to strengthen their relationship.

Irène was born on September 12, 1897, two years after Marie and Pierre Curie were married. Several weeks later, Pierre's father, a recent widower, came to live with them and take care of Irène when Marie was in the laboratory. Marie dressed and fed Irène in the morning, Grand Pé stayed with her during the days, and Marie took care of the baby in the evenings.

Irène proved to be a demanding child, and Marie an indulgent mother. Marie called her daughter "Little Queen" Irène and "the wild one." To keep the peace, Marie gave in to Irène's demands for tapioca pudding and her insistence on a particular type of apples. She sewed dresses for Irène and sat next to her crib until she fell asleep each night. If Irène woke up in the night, she would call *"Mé! Mé!"* until Marie returned to comfort her.

Irène Curie with Grand Pé — Pierre Curie's father, Dr. Eugène Curie — in 1903.

Even when she was with her daughter, thoughts about radium were never far from Marie's mind. Sometimes at night, after Irène was asleep, Marie and Pierre would leave Irène with her grandfather and take the 15-minute walk from their apartment to their laboratory. They would push open the creaking door to their workspace and stand in the darkness, marveling at the eerie blue-green glow coming from the test tubes and cups of radium on the tables. They stood in silence, staring in awe at radium, their "other baby." "These gleamings, which seemed suspended in darkness, stirred us with new emotion and enchantment," Marie wrote.

Marie described radium and radioactivity as "the child to whom she had given birth," one that she planned to nurture and devote herself to for "the whole of her working life." Marie loved her daughter, but Irène grew up with the clear understanding that her mother's research was also of great importance.

Grand Pé became a steady and reliable influence in Irène's life. He taught Irène to love science and nature, to question religion, and to embrace radical politics. As an adult, Irène said, "My spirit had been formed in great part by my grandfather Eugène, and my re-actions to political or religious questions came from him more than from my mother."

In terms of personality, Irène was very much like her father,

Marie Curie wrote that radium in the darkness looked "like faint, fairy lights."

Pierre: serious, curious, and ingenious. Irène typically spoke only when she had something meaningful to say, and she pondered questions carefully before reaching conclusions. She was socially awkward and never learned conventional manners. When Irène was a young girl, her mother invited students to the house for tea. Irène would hide behind her mother's skirt and periodically step out and demand, "You must take notice of me." When those same students tried to hug Irène or play with her hair, she would resist any form of affection, almost as if she wanted attention, but she wasn't sure what to do with it when she had it. On many occasions, her behavior was considered discourteous, but she never intended to be offensive or rude.

1903 Nobel Prize

In mid-November 1903, Marie and Pierre Curie received a telegram from the Royal Swedish Academy of Sciences notifying them that they, along with Henri Becquerel, had won the Nobel Prize for Physics. When reporters came to the house asking for interviews the following day, they found six-year-old Irène home alone. When asked where her parents were, she responded, "At the laboratory, of course." After the announcement of the prize, Irène had to share her parents not only with their work, but with the world as well. The press hounded the Curies at home and at work. For a few days, they posted one of their assistants at the door to keep reporters away so that they could do their research in peace. Although they did their best to downplay personal glorification, Marie and Pierre had become international celebrities, known not only for winning the Nobel Prize but also for discovering radium, a substance that was thought to be a miracle cure for cancer.

The cancer connection came about as a result of Pierre's

imagination and creative problem solving. In 1900, Pierre strapped a vial of radium salts to his forearm to see what would happen. After several hours, he removed the vial and found the site reddened and irritated. A few days later, an open sore appeared, and it took months for the wound to heal. "On the 42nd day, the epidermis began to re-form around the edges of the wound, approaching the center, and 52 days after the action of the rays, there is still an injury of one centimeter square with a grayish aspect indicating a deeper injury," Pierre wrote in his lab notes.

Pierre wondered what effect radium might have on skin cancer cells, so he began experimenting with mice, guinea pigs, rabbits, and, ultimately, people. He found that the cancerous tissue was destroyed by exposure to radiation, but that it grew back free of cancer. In June 1901, Pierre Curie and Becquerel issued a joint paper, "The Physiological Effects of Rays," in which they discussed how radium might be used to treat cancer. "Curietherapy," the use of radiation to treat cancer, began with doctors strapping vials of radioactive material to the surface of a patient's skin to shrink or eliminate tumors and cancerous lesions. While modern radiation treatment is far more refined in terms of targeting and dosing, the basic approach is essentially the same as it was more than 100 years ago. With this medical use of radium established, the Curies became even more famous.

Ironically, radium exposure made Marie, Pierre, Irène, and Frédéric quite sick throughout their lives. Researchers now know that low levels of radium exposure can cause fibrosis of the lungs, leukemia and other cancerous blood disorders, and damaged bone marrow and other conditions, but at the time, the Curies did not understand what radiation would do to their bodies.

When it came time to go to Stockholm for the Nobel Prize award ceremony, Marie and Pierre were both too sick to attend. It is impossible to know how much radiation the Curies were exposed to during their careers, but there is no doubt that they received dangerous levels of radiation every time they took a breath or touched their mouths in their workspace. Everything they ate or drank in their laboratory would have been contaminated with radioactive debris. Marie even slept with a small jar of radium at her bedside because she enjoyed staring at its eerie blue-green light before falling asleep. Even today, after more than 100 years, researchers who handle the Curies' papers and notebooks must wear protective clothing and sign a liability waiver because the items remain dangerously radioactive.

Marie and Pierre blamed their leg pains, weakness, fatigue, and overall poor health on their grueling schedules and physical labor. One undeniable consequence of handling radioactive materials was the damage to their fingertips. They both had painful, hardened fingertips that never completely healed. Until the end of her life, Marie rubbed her fingertips together to ease the constant pain.

An Unconventional Childhood

A few months after the Nobel Prize announcement, Marie conceived her second child. On December 6, 1904, when Irène was seven years old, her sister, Eve Denise Curie, was born. As they grew up, the differences between the sisters became evident. Irène was boorish and shy; Eve was charming and outgoing. Irène preferred to dress in loose, practical clothes; Eve had an eye for fashion. While both girls were intelligent, they were smart in different ways. Marie noted that Irène "resembled her father in intelligence. She was not as quick as her sister, but one could already see that she had a gift of reasoning power and that she would like science." In later years Irène became fascinated by physics and mathematics, while Eve studied piano and became a writer.

Irène and Ève Curie, 1906.

Marie and Pierre didn't believe the long hours and rote instruction of the traditional French educational system were effective. Marie believed that children should think more and memorize less, and that they should have plenty of time to play and make art and experiment in laboratories. With that in mind, when Irène was ten years old, Marie set up a private cooperative school with six other families, all with parents who taught at the university. Each family agreed to cover one class a week, so the work was divided and the children learned from experts in their field of study. When classes ended, the children and their teachers shared afternoon tea.

During the two and a half years the school operated, Irène made deep and trusted friendships that lasted the rest of her life. While she thrived academically, Irène never learned conventional social behaviors. She wasn't polite or courteous, she didn't understand the importance of small talk, and she saw no need to conform to social conventions. She refused to ask strangers "How do you do?" She turned away, uninterested, when something or someone bored her.

She was direct, honest, and engaged in what was going on around her. She spoke her mind—often bluntly, but always sincerely. She didn't like to waste time, and she ignored petty and mean people. These attitudes were reinforced and encouraged by her parents and Grand Pé. Irène didn't care about what most people wanted her to do; the only approval she sought was that of her family—especially her mother.

The cooperative school closed when parents' work schedules became too busy. Marie then enrolled Irène in a private school in Paris, where she became an excellent student and an avid reader in French, English, and German. "When I have a book," Irène said, "I devour it." Marie continued to tutor Irène in math.

During the summers, Marie sent Irène and Eve to vacation with Grand Pé while she stayed behind to work in the laboratory. When they were separated, Irène frequently wrote to her mother, begging her to join them. Most letters included algebra problems and solutions, as well as news of their activities. Even as a young girl, Irène knew that the easiest way for her to earn her mother's approval and keep her interest would be to share her passion for science and mathematics.

Some people thought Marie and Pierre's obsessive work habits and unbalanced lifestyle were a problem for their family. After seeing Marie and Pierre at a Physics Society meeting when Irène was a toddler, physicist Georges Sagnac, a colleague and a friend, wrote them a ten-page letter that read, in part:

> It is not necessary to mix scientific preoccupations into every instant of your life. . . . Don't you love Irène? It seems to me that I wouldn't prefer the idea of reading a paper by Rutherford to getting what my body needs and of looking at such an agreeable little girl. Give her a kiss for me. If she were a bit older, she would think as I do and she would tell you all this. Think of her a little.

Pierre didn't criticize Marie as a wife or mother, but he didn't help her out, either. He had a full appointment at the Sorbonne, so he left the domestic sphere to Marie. She did not resent Pierre for this, however: "He used to say that he had got a wife made expressly for him to share all his preoccupations." Referring to their shared passion for science, Marie continued, "Neither of us would contemplate abandoning that which was so precious to both."

Endings and Beginnings

In 1904, Pierre finally made his Nobel remarks in Stockholm to the Swedish Academy of Sciences; he spoke for both himself and Marie. Not surprisingly, he spoke about the power of radium:

> One can imagine that in criminal hands radium could become very dangerous, and here one must ask oneself if humanity gains anything by learning the secrets of nature, if humanity is ready to profit from this or whether such knowledge may not be destructive for it. The example of the discoveries of Nobel is characteristic. The powerful explosives

have enabled man to undertake some admirable works. They are also terrible means of destruction in the hands of great criminals who drag people toward war. I am one of those who think, like Nobel, that humanity will draw more good than evil from new discoveries.

He knew that their discovery was a vital link in the chain of scientific evolution, although he probably never imagined the possibility of an atomic bomb.

Pierre's career continued to thrive, which meant he had even less time for Irène. He had been appointed a professor of physics at the Faculty of Sciences of the University of Paris. At last he had funds for several paid workers and a laboratory. He hired Marie as laboratory chief; it was the first time she had received pay for research. But just as their lives should have become more financially and professionally secure, tragedy struck.

On Wednesday, April 19, 1906, Pierre Curie attended a luncheon meeting, then walked down the Rue Dauphine toward the river Seine. A steady rain forced him to hide under a big black umbrella. The hypnotizing sound of the rain thumping against the umbrella may have made it hard for him to hear the hoofbeats of the heavy horse-drawn carriage loaded with military uniforms that was clattering along the narrow road.

Pierre Curie in 1906, the year he died.

Absentminded and lost in thought, Pierre did not look before stepping out into the middle of the street, directly into the path of the oncoming horses. The horses stepped over him, but he slipped and fell. The carriage wheel crushed his skull. Pierre died instantly.

When Marie returned home from the laboratory later that night, Pierre's father told her what had happened. Eight-year-old Irène was next door playing with a friend. Marie—suddenly the single parent of two small children—told Irène that her father had been in an accident and needed rest. She couldn't bring herself to tell Irène the truth; not yet.

In the days that followed, Irène remained under a neighbor's care while Marie tended to the funeral arrangements. Pierre was buried in the French countryside where he grew up. The service included no religious rites or prayers, and when it was over Marie stood by her husband's burial site, plucked the flowers off a bouquet, and methodically spread them over his grave.

After the funeral, Marie went to the neighbor's house to tell Irène the truth: Her father was dead. Irène listened to what her mother said, but continued playing as if she had not heard the words. As Marie prepared to return home, she said to her friend, "She is too young to understand." Irène burst into tears and ran to her mother for comfort; she did understand.

That summer, Marie's sister Helena, or Hela, took Irène and Eve to the seashore, giving Marie time to be alone. Irène longed to see her mother, but she was told she would have to wait. Two months after Pierre's death, Marie's sister Bronislana, or Bronya, came to stay with her. Bronya found Marie on a hot June day in front of a roaring fire. Marie took a wrapped bundle from an armoire and opened the package. It held a heap of muddy, bloody rags. At first Bronya was confused, but then she realized that the scraps were the clothes that Pierre had been wearing when he died. Marie cut them into pieces and threw them one by one into the fire. When Marie kissed the last strips, Bronya pulled them away and tossed them into the fire. Bronya held her sister while she cried. The next day, Marie was cool and composed.

Marie's good-bye ritual helped her move on, but from that point forward, Marie never wanted to hear Pierre's name mentioned again. At times, Irène tried to talk to her mother about her father, but Marie ended the conversations abruptly, and Irène didn't want to upset her mother by pressing the issue. Irène had lost her father to the grave and her mother to grief. Grand Pé still lived with the family; he recognized how difficult things were for Irène, so he paid special attention to her and kept her going day after day, with the hope that sooner or later things would feel normal again.

More Time Without Mé

In 1910, when Irène was thirteen years old, Grand Pé died after a year-long illness. Irène had a hard time adjusting to his death. That summer she and Eve went again to the seashore with their Aunt Hela, but Irène found it difficult to relax. Marie made a brief visit to the shore, then returned to her work in Paris. Irène wrote a series of sad and anxious letters to her mother: "WHEN ARE YOU COMING BACK? . . . I shall be so happy when you come because I badly need someone to caress . . . I have made a fine paper envelope to hold your letters. There is only one in it."

Later that summer Irène wrote to her mother again: "I love you very much, you see, and I would like you to come. Come quickly or at least write me when you are coming. Your BIGGG Irène is impatient to see you again." She continued that her vacation would be better "if a sweet Mé were here, near me, to look at." Despite Irène's pleading, Marie did not visit her children again that summer.

The following year brought more strife to the Curie family. Marie decided to compete in the election of a single open seat at the prestigious French Academy of Sciences, the most powerful organization in French science. New members were elected only when an existing Academy member died, so openings were rare. Marie competed for the spot against another scientist, who engaged in a campaign that characterized Marie as a liberal, feminist foreigner, since she had immigrated from Poland to attend college. Marie lost the election by just two votes. The issue became so heated that the Academy held a follow-up vote, which barred women from eligibility for any future openings. (The first woman wasn't elected to the Academy until 1979.)

There was more bad publicity to come. In the fall of 1911, Marie traveled to Brussels to attend the first international Solvay Conference with several dozen of the world's top physicists, including Paul Langevin, a 39-year-old married father of four and expert in molecular and kinetic theory. Langevin was a long-standing family friend and one of Pierre's former students—and he and Marie were having a love affair.

In early November, Irène was at home and her mother was attending the conference when news of the affair became public. The headline in one of the French newspapers read: "A Story of Love: Madame Curie and Professor Langevin." Some accounts report that when Irène read about her mother's affair, she fainted from shock.

Three days later, while still at the conference, Marie received a telegram announcing that she had won a second Nobel Prize. Not only was she the first woman to receive

Irène Curie touches her mother's radium-scarred fingertips in 1908. Throughout her childhood, Irène longed to spend more time with her mother.

the prize in the sciences, she was now the first person—male or female—to win it twice, first in physics and the second time in chemistry. (Pierre might have shared the second prize with Marie, but the Nobel Prize cannot be awarded posthumously.)

The Nobel news intensified attention on the scandal around Marie's personal life. The Nobel committee had reservations about presenting the award to a woman involved in a romantic scandal. Several scientists organized a campaign to get Marie to refuse the award. Other colleagues stood by Marie. As planned, Marie attended the ceremony in December 1911 with Bronya and 14-year-old Irène.

Irène proudly watched her mother receive a second Nobel Prize, but after they returned to Paris, Marie fell into a deep de-

Publicity about Marie Curie's relationship with Paul Langevin peaked when a Parisian newspaper published their personal correspondence and characterized Curie as being "an ambitious Pole who had ridden to glory on [Pierre] Curie's coattails and was now trying to latch onto Langevin's." In response, Langevin challenged the newspaper editor to a duel to defend Marie's honor. During the showdown, neither man pulled a weapon.

pression. What should have been a time of celebration and pride for Marie became a period of humiliation and shame. She returned to angry mobs throwing rocks at her windows and yelling: "Go home to Poland." Her romantic relationship with Langevin ended, although they remained friends and colleagues for the rest of their lives.

For the next year, Marie remained in seclusion in the French countryside, traveling under her maiden name or using Bronya's name because she feared that she had sullied her husband's reputation. Irène and Eve stayed in Paris with a Polish nurse and saw very little of their mother for more than a year. Much to her dismay, when Irène wrote to her mother, she was told to address the envelope to "Manya Sklodowska." Marie Curie was gone—at least for a while.

During the time her mother was away, Irène continued her studies and tried to protect her mother's privacy. She blamed the press for her mother's heartache, and she became more distrustful of people she did not know. Irène still longed for her mother's approval and her attention, but there was nothing for her to do but wait until her mother was able to make time for her.

ON THE BATTLEFIELDS

IRÈNE CURIE YEARNED for more time with her mother, but she had to endure another extended separation in the summer of 1914. This time the problem wasn't personal but political: In June a Serbian student assassinated Archduke Franz Ferdinand, heir to the throne of Austria-Hungary. Fighting broke out, and the war escalated quickly; within weeks, French men were being drafted for military service. Marie thought her children would be safer in the countryside than the city, so she sent 16-year-old Irène and 9-year-old Eve from Paris to a villa in northwest France in the care of two Polish maids.

Irène looked forward to early August when Marie planned to join them in L'Arcouest, but when the date approached their reunion was put off again. The fighting was growing more intense, and Marie decided to stay in Paris to defend her laboratories. "If I am there, perhaps the Germans will not dare plunder them; but if I go away, everything will disappear," Marie said.

As weeks passed and the situation became less stable, Marie worried that communication with her children would become impossible. On August 28, 1914, Marie wrote to Irène:

> [We] are beginning to face the possibility of a siege of Paris, in which case we might be cut off. If that should happen, endure it with courage, for our personal desires are nothing in comparison with the great struggle that is now underway. You must feel responsible for your sister and take care of her if we should be separated for a longer time than I expected.

Several days later, Marie wrote again:

> Things are not going very well, and we are all heavyhearted and disturbed in soul. We need great courage, and I hope that we shall not lack it. We must keep our certainty that after the bad days the good times will come again. It is in this hope that I press you to my heart, my beloved daughters.

Irène did not find comfort in her mother's words. She knew that Marie was trying to keep her safe, but what Irène really wanted was the comfort of being near her mother. Irène begged to join her mother in Paris once more, but Marie refused.

On September 6, 1914, Marie wrote to Irène again: "My sweet dear . . . I sense how you have already become a companion and friend to me. If you cannot work for France today, work for its future. Many people will be missing after this war; it will be necessary to replace them." She concluded her letter, "Do your physics and mathematics as best you can." As usual, she included several algebraic problems to keep Irène's mind engaged.

Irène's Homecoming

By September, the French had stopped the German march toward Paris. Once the situation had stabilized, Marie sent for Irène and Eve. Just before she was to come home, Irène injured her foot while rock climbing with friends. Although she was frustrated by the delay, Irène approached the experience with curiosity. "I was rather amused," Irène wrote to her mother about the injury.

> First I established that the view of my foot didn't bother me at all, and that gave me pleasure because I had often wondered if I was afraid of the sight of blood. I looked at my wound with much interest because one could see the tendon. I also saw how they put in the clips [to hold the wound together]. Naturally, with each clip they put in (or took out if it was badly placed), I stiffened in order not to cry, but in the intervals, I laughed and I joked a lot better than all my audience gathered around.

After a two-week delay to give her foot a chance to heal, Irène returned to Paris, confident that seeing blood and injury would not stop her from becoming a nurse.

As soon as she arrived home, Irène enrolled in a nursing course. She also helped her mother move from her old laboratory to the newly opened Radium Institute, a state-of-the-art research facility built by the University of Paris and the Pasteur Institute. In her free time, Irène cataloged her mother's scientific journals and classified various specimens of radioactive materials.

By fall 1914, Irène had completed her nurse's training and proved that she was ready to join her mother at the front, teaching doctors and nurses how to use X-ray equipment. Their shared experiences near the battlefields would bring Marie and Irène closer together. From that point forward, they would no longer interact just as mother and daughter; they would be colleagues as well.

X-Rays on the Front Lines

When the war began, Marie realized how important X-ray technology could be to wounded soldiers by helping to pinpoint the exact nature and location of their battlefield injuries. At the time, few French hospitals had X-ray machines, and those that did were not located near the battlefields, where they were needed most. Marie had never worked with X-rays herself, but she was familiar with them in concept because of her work with radioactivity, and she knew that they could be used to save lives.

Marie used her status as a well-known and respected scientist with two Nobel Prizes to launch the X-ray program. She persuaded the French government to allow her to set up both mobile and permanent military radiological centers. Within ten days of the troops mobilizing at the start of the war, Marie took a leave of absence from her work at the Sorbonne and was named the director of the newly formed Red Cross Radiology Service.

Marie convinced wealthy people to donate their cars, X-ray manufacturers to donate their equipment, and automobile repair shops to donate their skills to modify the cars for use as mobile X-ray stations. Since there was no reliable source of electricity on the battlefield, Marie had dynamos—electric generators—installed in the vehicles so that the car engines could be used to power the X-ray machines.

Although it was a challenging task, by November 1 the first of these specialized mobile X-ray vehicles was ready for service. It was a hand-cranked Renault truck, painted Army gray with a Red Cross logo on each side, and a maximum speed of just 20 miles per hour—nothing fancy, but it worked. The French enlisted men called the trucks "petite Curies"—little Curies—in Marie's honor.

By the time the car was ready to go, so was Irène. She had received enough training at nursing school and from her mother to be of use as an X-ray technician, and she figured she would learn anything else she needed to know on the job. Marie and Irène's first trip was to a bombed-out building that served as a military field hospital in Creil, about 20 miles behind the front line in northern France.

Irène Curie stepping from a mobile X-ray unit in 1916. During the four years of World War I, more than one million French soldiers were assessed using X-ray technology.

When they arrived, the head surgeon told them they weren't needed; he didn't believe in X-rays.

Instead of debating with the man, Marie and Irène quietly went to work. They unloaded their equipment, showed the nurses how to black out the windows using curtains and tape, and within about a half hour of their arrival they began seeing patients. Marie and Irène demonstrated how to pass a scope over the body to survey it for injury. In extreme emergencies, the doctor operated immediately, but more often X-ray pictures were taken of the areas that needed special attention.

Understanding the X-rays required the use of basic geometry. Irène and Marie taught the doctors and nurses how to perform the calculations necessary to identify the exact location of an injury.

Typically, the surgeons started out as skeptics, only to be converted into absolute believers in the use of X-rays once they saw how useful they were.

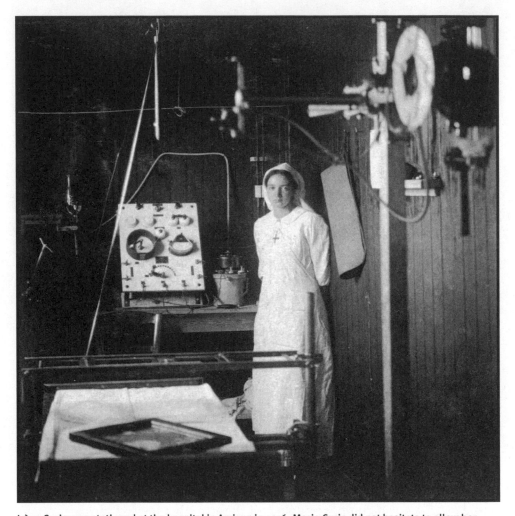

Irène Curie was stationed at the hospital in Amiens in 1916. Marie Curie did not hesitate to allow her daughter to help as an X-ray technician. "My mother had no more doubts about me than she doubted herself," Irène said after the war.

On the Job

From the first day on the job, Irène wanted to prove herself and make her mother proud, so she refused to be intimidated by the death and gore that surrounded her. She had to be tough; there was no room for fear or second thoughts. She did not falter when she heard grown men crying out in pain, begging for help, calling out that they wanted to see their wives and children one more time before they died. She did not slow down when she saw military officers come to the hospitals to pin medals on dying soldiers, both to thank them for their service and to ensure that their survivors would receive a widow's pension. Irène did not allow the horror of war to unnerve her: She had a job to do, and she did it.

Marie approved of Irène's iron will and stoic disposition. Irène always displayed courage and confidence, calmly performing whatever task her mother assigned. Irène emulated her famous mother's manner, borrowing from her strength. Mother and daughter were not insensitive to suffering; they had learned how to detach themselves from the agony around them enough to treat their patients and keep good records.

Irène also learned how to interact with patients and to treat them with compassion by watching her mother. When soldiers worried that the X-ray would hurt, Marie offered a comforting smile and reassured them that the procedure wouldn't hurt any more than having a photograph taken.

For months, Irène and her mother did the same when they arrived at a new field hospital to offer their services. Their success brought increased demand, and over time twenty additional vehicles were converted into radiological trucks. In addition to the portable units, Irène and the other X-ray technicians helped set up two hundred permanent radiological posts inside hospitals during the course of the war.

Irène Curie and the other X-ray nurses camped near the hospital while stationed in Hoogstade, Belgium, in 1915. In the field, Irène and her mother lived like soldiers, eating the same rations and sleeping whenever and wherever they could.

After a year traveling as her mother's assistant, Irène began to work on her own in the fall of 1916. Like her mother, when Irène encountered challenges or opposition from the military she did not to take "no" for an answer. She once traveled by train to a large military hospital in Amiens to install an X-ray unit at a hospital there. When she arrived, she found the city in chaos following an air raid. The military authorities told Irène that they wouldn't be able to unpack her equipment for more than two weeks, so she would have to wait.

As she had seen her mother do on many occasions, Irène ignored the official and went to work. Irène, a sergeant, and a medical student unpacked the railroad car and installed the X-ray equipment on their own. Within an hour, Irène slipped on a pair of cotton gloves and stepped behind a wooden screen—the only protection she used to shield herself from the harmful X-rays—and she started to see patients. As Irène later said, when necessary she "surmounted the little difficulties of the moment."

Irène encountered a particularly disagreeable surgeon when working alone in Hoogstade, Belgium. Before beginning a procedure, she had done a detailed analysis of a patient's leg. The ghostly black-and-white images she had seen revealed the clear outline of metal shrapnel and bone in the shadow of the French soldier's wounded thigh. The doctor did not bother to read Irène's report and he did not want to use the X-ray equipment, so he prepared to enter the wound from the front. Irène urged the surgeon to explore the wound from the other side, but the doctor ignored her. He was a veteran physician with years of experience, and he had no intention of taking medical advice from a 17-year-old nurse with an X-ray machine. Instead, he picked up his forceps and probed the gaping wound in the soldier's thigh, searching for the bullet fragment hidden somewhere inside his patient's flesh.

Irène listened to the young man's groans and cries as the surgeon explored his wound without success. Artillery fire blasted the front lines just a few miles away. More wounded would be coming. Irène wanted to speak up—to show the doctor where to look—but she remained silent. Eventually, the frustrated surgeon turned toward Irène for help. She showed him where he should enter the wound. He followed her advice and promptly located the offending piece of shrapnel. From that point forward, he willingly used X-rays as a guide.

Irène celebrated her 18th birthday in September 1916 at the post in Hoogstade, Belgium. "I spent my birthday admirably," she wrote to her mother. "Except that you weren't there."

Not long after her birthday, Irène returned to Paris to continue her studies at the Sorbonne. She was late starting classes in the fall of 1916 because she was needed on the battlefield, but she had no trouble making up the missed work. She then split her time between taking classes at the university and training new X-ray technicians at the Curie Institute.

MORE THAN SKIN DEEP

During World War I, Irène Curie and other X-ray technicians used two technologies to obtain images of their patients: radiography (film images) and fluoroscopy (real-time moving images).

Radiography recorded the images on a piece of film housed inside a wooden frame. The patient held the film in place while exposed to the X-ray. In the early days, it could take ten minutes or longer to make an exposure, and the patient couldn't move or the image would be blurred.

In most battlefield situations, it proved to be more efficient and effective to use fluoroscopy. Fluoroscopy required a patient to lie on an examining table outfitted with an X-ray source mounted underneath it. As the X-rays passed through the table and through the patient's body, they lost some intensity, which created the classic shadowy images associated with an X-ray image. The doctor or X-ray technician wore a fluoroscope, which looked like a swim mask with a screen coated in a fluorescent chemical that glowed when the X-rays struck it. A real-time X-ray image appeared on the screen, so there was no need to take pictures and develop films, making it faster and easier for the user to calculate the depth of a bullet and its relation to the entry wound.

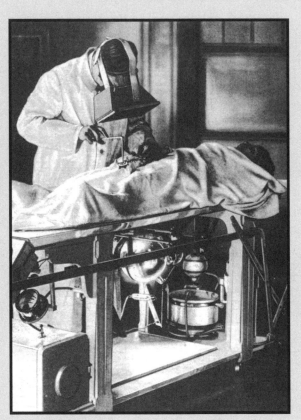

A doctor using a fluoroscope to examine an injured soldier during World War I.

Until the war ended in November 1918, Irène kept up with her studies, occasionally joining her mother at the front whenever time permitted. A map of France was posted on the dining room wall so that Irène and Eve could place little flags on it to trace their mother's journey along the front.

Amazingly, during this time Irène managed to complete three degrees, with distinction, from the Sorbonne: mathematics in 1915, physics in 1916, and chemistry in 1917. Irène continued her education not only because she was intellectually curious, but because it brought her one step closer to her ultimate goal: She wanted to join her mother as a researcher at the Radium Institute when the war ended.

4

DR. AND MRS.

FTER WORLD WAR I ended, Irène became her mother's assistant at the Radium Institute, while also working on her doctorate from the Sorbonne. Like her mother, Irène was hypnotized by radium's radioactive glow, and she said that its otherworldly shimmer made her feel like an adventurer or explorer. Work never bored her; she delighted in every unexpected discovery or colorful precipitate that settled to the bottom of a test tube.

While many French women at the time defined themselves through their roles as wives and mothers, Irène focused her attention on scientific pursuits. Irène's coworkers in the laboratory called her the "Crown Princess of Science" and some felt jealous of her privileged status in her mother's institute. Irène made no effort to gain her coworkers' acceptance. Many of them thought she was conceited and entitled. She spoke bluntly. One colleague said: "Irène not only called a spade a spade but felt free to analyze the spade's defects." Irène's sister, Eve, described Irène's directness in more favorable terms. She said: "I never heard her say a bad thing, and, to my knowledge, she has never lied in her life. She is exactly what she

The Radium Institute was built by the University of Paris and the Pasteur Institute between 1909 and 1914, but it was not occupied until after the end of World War I. The building now houses the Curie Museum, which was established in 1934 after Marie Curie's death.

shows us, with all her merits and demerits, without embellishing anything to please us."

Irène didn't smile much at work, although she expressed joy easily when she was with her family and close friends. She had a disconcerting habit of lifting up her lab coat and skirt in the middle of a conversation to pull a dirty handkerchief out from a petticoat pocket so that she could loudly blow her nose. She wore unfashionable baggy dresses with loose waistbands and open sleeves so that she could move around easily. She felt no need to justify her behavior or explain herself. She didn't care what anyone thought about her, with the exception of her mother: Even as an adult, Irène strived to please her mother. Irène once wrote about their relationship: "I was very

Marie Curie taught Irène everything she knew about working with radioactive substances.

different from her, more like my father, and that's perhaps one of the reasons that we got along so well."

Before she married, Irène lived with her mother and sister. Every morning Irène would make breakfast and sit with her mother and discuss books, poetry, and the theater, as well as news from the lab. Marie appreciated Irène's companionship; she wrote to her daughter: "You know, my child, that you are an excellent friend for me and that you make my life easier and sweeter. I look forward to work with more courage, thinking of your smile and your ever joyous face."

When not in the laboratory, Irène spent a lot of time outdoors. She was tall and fit and energetic. She sometimes stayed out late dancing, and she and a friend took two-week hiking trips in the mountains every summer. She swam in the river Seine, skied in the French Alps, and took pleasure testing her physical limits.

On Tour in America

The Curie family remained an enigma to many. Journalists still hounded Marie Curie for interviews, but she almost never agreed. When Marie "Missy" Meloney, editor of the American women's magazine *The Delineator*, asked her French colleague Stéphanie

Irène Curie hiking at Le Monêtier-les-Bains in southeastern France in 1931.

Lauzanne for tips on how to approach Marie, Lauzanne told her, "She will see no one."

In May 1920, Meloney asked Marie for an interview anyway; she refused. Instead of taking no for an answer, Meloney wrote again, explaining: "You have been important to me for twenty years, and I want to see you for a few minutes." Something about that request resonated with Marie. She agreed to see Meloney the following day.

The two women got along well from the start. In their conversation, Marie explained how she and Pierre thought it would be wrong to profit from the discovery of radium, even though they knew that chemical manufacturing companies would make a fortune from their discovery. (They were correct: At the time, there were only 140 grams of radium in existence worldwide—not even enough to fill two tablespoons—and the Standard Chemical Company of Pittsburgh had produced more than half of it. Each gram was worth $150,000, about $2 million in today's dollars. It was expensive to produce because there were no shortcuts to the labor-intensive process Marie and Pierre had developed.)

Meloney immediately realized that she had a great story to tell. With Marie's approval, Meloney launched a campaign to have the women of the United States buy a gram of radium for Marie Curie. As part of the fundraising program, Marie and her daughters—Irène, 23, and Eve, 16—would tour the United States and talk about her work.

The April 1921 issue of *The Delineator* featured several stories about Marie, including the lead article, "The Greatest Woman in the World." In May, Marie, Irène, and Eve arrived in New York City, where they were greeted by thousands of cheering fans. Marie and Irène were horrified at the attention. They did not know how to handle their sudden celebrity.

As part of the six-week tour, Marie accepted more than twenty honorary degrees and attended an opening reception at Carnegie Hall in New York City and a closing ceremony at the White

House with President Warren G. Harding.

Each of the Curies responded differently to the tour. Eve, who reporters called "Miss Radium Eyes," loved the excitement. Marie found the attention overwhelming, and Irène took it all in and brought along a book so that she could read when she got bored. In her silk stockings and French fashions, Eve looked the part of the Parisian sophisticate. Irène, on the other hand, wore baggy dresses, sensible shoes, and cotton stockings; the press often de-scribed her as looking "peasant-like."

Missy Meloney wrote: "I had been prepared to meet a woman of the world, enriched by her own efforts . . . but Madame Curie was a simple woman, working in an inadequate laboratory and living in an inexpensive apartment." Marie Curie's modesty impressed Meloney and those who donated to her campaign to raise $150,000 to buy a gram of radium for the Radium Institute. Pictured left to right: Missy Meloney, Irène Curie, Marie Curie, and Eve Curie.

Irène sometimes stood in for her mother at speaking engage-ments and ceremonies when Marie was too tired to participate. Even with Irène as her surrogate, there were times when Marie could not bring herself to shake hands with more enthusiastic admirers, so she pretended to be injured and wore a sling on her arm to avoid receiv-ing lines. Throughout the trip, Irène proved to be a worthy stand-in for her mother, and she demonstrated that she shared her mother's passion for the study of radioactivity.

Irène Curie stood in for her mother and accepted an honorary degree from the University of Pennsylvania in 1921. Irène received her own doctorate four years later from the Sorbonne in Paris.

Another Dr. Curie

During the time she was working at the Radium Institute, Irène prepared her doctoral dissertation, an analysis of the alpha particles emitted by polonium as it decays. Specifically, Irène focused on the way the particles slowed as they move through matter. Her mother had discovered polonium in 1898 when Irène was a year old, and the element had proven to be essential for atomic research. Irène dedicated her dissertation: "To Madame Curie by her daughter and pupil."

In 1925, Irène went to the Sorbonne to defend her dissertation by answering questions about her research in an amphitheater crowded with spectators. After she presented a brief summary of her work, a group of her professors asked her questions about her research. She was not nervous; she saw no reason to be since she was well prepared and no one knew her subject better than she did. One person was notably absent from the event: Marie Curie. She stayed at the laboratory to avoid upstaging her daughter.

Afterward, Marie hosted a tea in Irène's honor in the garden at the Radium Institute. Tables were set up outside, and she served cookies on developing trays from the photo darkroom. The tea was heated in laboratory flasks over Bunsen burners and served in beakers with glass stirring rods rather than teacups and spoons. Irène was delighted.

Irène's achievement was reported in newspapers around the world. A female French journalist interviewed Irène and asked if a career in physics might be too difficult for a woman.

"Not at all," Irène replied. "I believe that men's and women's scientific aptitudes are exactly the same. . . . A woman of science should renounce worldly obligations. . . ."

"And what about family obligations?" asked the reporter.

"These are possible on the condition that they are accepted as additional burdens . . . for my part, I consider science to be the paramount interest of my life."

One of Irène's colleagues at the Radium Institute in attendance at the tea party—Frédéric Joliot—may have been pleased to hear Irène say that there was room in her life for family. Since he had started working at the Institute the year before, the two had moved from coworkers to friends, and both considered the possibility that their relationship could turn into something more permanent.

The Joliot-Curies

Frédéric Joliot grew up idolizing Marie and Pierre Curie. As a boy, he set up a makeshift chemistry lab in the family bathroom, and on the wall he hung pictures of the Curies that he had cut out of magazines. In December 1924, Frédéric went to the Radium Institute to interview for a position in the lab. When he finally met Marie, she was much smaller than he expected; in his mind, she was a giant.

Paul Langevin had been Frédéric's professor in college, and he recommended the 24-year-old for the job. Marie hired Frédéric on the spot and sent him to Irène to teach him the basics of working with radioactive materials.

Irène, who was three years older, paid Frédéric little attention initially. At first he thought she didn't like him because she didn't say "hello" to him when she arrived at work in the mornings. Irène didn't greet anyone; it never occurred to her.

At first glance, the two seemed to have little in common: Frédéric was outgoing and charming; Irène was introverted and awkward. He put other people at ease; she made other people uncomfortable. He worried about what other people thought of him; she missed many social cues and didn't care about other people's opinions of her.

Their daughter, Hélène, considered her parents "opposites at *everything*." She said:

> Relationships between people were important to him; he would guess quickly if someone had a problem, and he wanted others to understand him. Mother could walk right through something and see nothing. If somebody didn't shake hands with him, he'd worry; my mother wouldn't have noticed. Connections with people were tighter and more complicated with him; they were a nuisance for my mother. My mother was very like Pierre Curie, more stable. She needed time to think, and she'd do only what she wanted.

Despite their different dispositions, as Irène and Frédéric got to know each other, they found that they shared a love of sports, a passion for antiwar politics, and, most importantly, a lifelong devotion to science.

Frédéric Joliot at the time he applied for a position at the Radium Institute in Paris.

Frédéric began lingering after work, pretending he needed to ask Irène a question, then walking her home. This became a habit, and then they began sharing time outdoors on weekends. Frédéric said:

> I discovered in this girl, who other people regarded some-
> what as a block of ice, an extraordinary person, sensitive and
> poetic, who in many things gave the impression of being a
> living replica of what her father had been. I had read much
> about Pierre Curie. I had heard teachers who had known
> him talking about him and I rediscovered in his daughter the
> same purity, his good sense, his humility.

It was not long before Irène announced to her mother that she was getting married.

Irène and Frédéric married on October 9, 1926. After a civil cer-emony, they had lunch at Marie's apartment and spent the afternoon working at the lab—what they considered an ideal day.

At first, Marie was a difficult mother-in-law. She resented Frédéric for taking Irène away from her. In Irène's words: "When I married, my mother was certainly pained to find us partly sepa-rated." She was right. Marie wrote to her brother: "I miss Irène a lot. We were so close for such a long time. Of course, we often see each other, but it's not the same." Marie didn't fully trust Frédéric in the beginning. She insisted that Irène obtain a prenuptial agreement, and she ensured that Irène—not Frédéric—would someday inherit the use of the radium at the Institute. For the first few years of their marriage, Marie introduced Frédéric to strangers as "the man who married Irène."

Over time, though, Marie became very fond of Frédéric. He and Irène ate dinner with Marie several nights a week, and mother-in-law and son-in-law formed a relationship of their own. Soon Irène found herself complaining: "My mother and my husband talked often with such ardor, with such rapidity, that I could never say a word. " Marie began to respect Frédéric's abilities as a scientist, and, ultimately, she took great pride in his accomplishments. "The boy is a skyrocket," she said.

In the early years of their marriage, Irène's reputation and scientific skill surpassed Frédéric's, just as Marie's noteworthy career had made it difficult for her daughter to emerge from her shadows. Some called Frédéric "The Prince Consort," assuming that he had married Irène to further his career. Even after ten years of marriage, the rumors persisted. Frédéric asked a colleague: "Why are people so nasty? Why do they claim that I don't love my wife and that I have married her just for the sake of my career? But I do love my wife. I love her very much."

Frédéric's use of the name Joliot-Curie may have fueled the criticism. At the time, it was customary for a woman to take a man's surname when they married. Irène had established a strong reputation and she had published articles in scientific journals before her marriage, so she decided to continue to use her maiden name professionally. Instead of using Joliot as the family name, Frédéric encouraged the use of the name Joliot-Curie. They signed many scientific papers as "Irène Curie" and "F. Joliot." They signed other articles and political statements as "Joliot-Curie," and socially they were often simply "Joliot." Irène didn't care which name they used, but Frédéric did.

A colleague once told Frédéric that he didn't need to use the Curie name to bolster his reputation. Frédéric said, "Funny, you have a bee in your bonnet about it. You're like my daughter. She's always telling me: 'Don't call yourself Curie.' " When he referred to himself with a hyphenated name, a journalist wrote: "M. Frédéric Joliot-Curie is certainly a great man, but not sufficiently so, it seems, to be called simply Joliot." The name issue was never resolved. At the end of his life, Frédéric thought about formally changing the family name to "Joliot-Curie" so the hyphenated version would live on after he was gone.

A year after Irène and Frédéric were married, Irène gave birth to their first child, Hélène. At that time, doctors told Irène that she had

Irène Joliot-Curie with her daughter, Hélène, who grew up to become a nuclear physicist and professor at the Institute of Nuclear Physics, University of Paris. Hélène's brother, Pierre, became a noted biophysicist.

tuberculosis and she should not have any more children. Instead of complying, she returned to work and had a second child, Pierre, named for her father, a few years later.

Both personally and professionally, Frédéric and Irène worked well together. Frédéric was a physicist with doctoral work in chemistry; Irène was a chemist with doctoral work in physics. Frédéric had an agile mind that took multiple perspectives into consideration; Irène had a methodical mind that systematically worked through each alternative when problem solving. They complemented one another, each stronger for the other's contributions.

They soon earned a reputation as a powerful research team. They were young, well educated, and they had access to one of the finest physics labs in the world. Irène and Frédéric were coming of age during the Golden Age of Physics, a time in the early 1930s when research teams around the world were making significant strides in understanding the way the world worked. During this fruitful period of exploration and collaboration, scientists openly shared their experimental results, and almost every new edition of the physics journals brought news of original ideas and theories and discoveries. The world of physics was exploding with exciting possibilities and, at least for that moment, nothing seemed impossible.

RIGHT ON TIME

THE RACE WAS on. During the early days of the 1930s, physicists around the world were competing with each other to be the first to discover and then document new ideas and insights. One idea fueled another, making this an extremely productive and inspiring period of scientific advancement.

For the most part, researchers worked in small teams and published their work for the benefit of all. Some of the key players in this international race for knowledge were Frédéric and Irène Joliot-Curie at the Radium Institute in Paris, France; Lise Meitner and Otto Hahn at the Kaiser Wilhelm Institute in Berlin, Germany; Ernest Rutherford and James Chadwick at the Cavendish Laboratory in Cambridge, England; Enrico Fermi and his team of six researchers at the University of Rome in Italy; and Niels Bohr at the Institute of Theoretical Physics in Copenhagen, Denmark. With such fierce competition to be first to make a discovery, many researchers felt the need to hasten their pace and to publish their work as quickly as possible.

When Irène and Frédéric did their first presentation at the Solvay Conference in 1933, some of their colleagues wondered if they had been working too fast, rushing to make a name for themselves. This concern was not entirely unfounded. In recent years, Irène and Frédéric had overlooked two important scientific discoveries that they believed they should have made.

Too Late: Missing the Neutron

In the first case, Irène had been inspired by the work of German physicists Walter Bothe and Herbert Becker. Bothe and Becker did an experiment in which they placed a radioactive substance next to a non-radioactive substance to see what would happen. In the experiment, Bothe bombarded the lightweight metal beryllium with particles from radioactive polonium. The experiment generated an unexpectedly powerful form of radiation.

After reading about Bothe and Becker's work, Irène and Frédéric conducted a follow-up study of what they thought were new rays. First, they repeated Bothe's experiment. As expected, they found that the beryllium gave off powerful rays—they could even force their way through lead. Next, the Joliot-Curies placed other substances in the path of the rays to see what would happen. They found that when the rays passed through paraffin wax, the protons from the wax accelerated and shot out at a speed equal to one-tenth of the speed of light. Why would the protons blast out of the paraffin with so much power?

Irène and Frédéric knew that other research teams were working on the same issue. Eager to come up with a theory as quickly as possible, the Joliot-Curies theorized—incorrectly—that the experiment had produced powerful gamma rays. In January 1932, they published that conclusion in an article titled "The Emission of Protons of Great Speed . . . Under the Influence of Gamma Rays."

Not everyone who read the article thought the Joliot-Curies' conclusions were correct. Ernest Rutherford dismissed their findings as impossible: "I don't believe it," he said. Gamma rays have no mass and could not make heavy particles move that fast, he argued.

Additional research showed that the Joliot-Curies had been wrong. They had not found gamma rays. They did not understand their own data, which instead showed that they had produced proof that neutrons exist. Another researcher later made the discovery. Rutherford had been skeptical of the Joliot-Curies' findings, so he asked his colleague, James Chadwick, to look into the matter. Chadwick repeated Irène and Frédéric's experiment, becoming more and more involved in the project. During a 10-day period, he worked around the clock, pausing to sleep only about three hours each night. He knew he was on to something important.

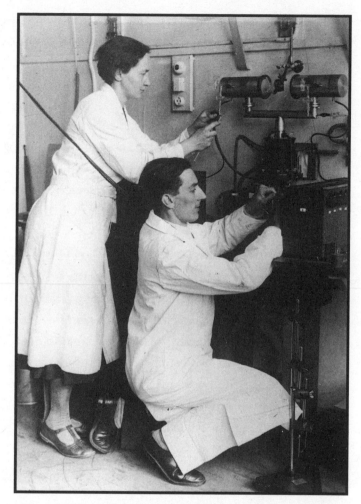

Irène and Frédéric Joliot-Curie working at the Radium Institute in 1932.

"A few days of strenuous work were sufficient to show that these strange effects were due to a neutral particle and to enable me to measure its mass: The neutron postulated by Rutherford in 1920 had at last revealed itself," Chadwick said. While Rutherford thought that a neutral particle must exist in the atom's nucleus, Chadwick was the first to prove it. One month after the Joliot-Curies published their research, Chadwick published an article titled "Possible Existence of the Neutron" in the journal *Nature*. In 1935 he won the Nobel Prize in Physics for discovering the neutron.

Irène and Frédéric were frustrated that they had let this discovery slip past them. "It is annoying to be overtaken by other laboratories which immediately take up one's experiments," Frédéric later wrote about this period of his research life. In public, however, he was gracious about congratulating Chadwick for his good work. Chadwick acknowledged that he was not the first to produce neutrons—pointing out that the Joliot-Curies had conducted similar experiments before—but he was the first to correctly interpret his experimental findings. According to Italian physicist Emilio Segrè, Chadwick's achievement was to recognize neutrons for what they were "immediately, clearly, and convincingly." The fact that the Joliot-Curies had come so close to discovering the neutron only because they misunderstood their data was both embarrassing and disappointing.

Then the same mistake happened again.

Too Late Again: Missing the Positron

The discovery of the neutron changed the understanding of physics, and it opened new areas of research. Neutrons help to stabilize the nucleus by binding with protons and with each other. Once scientists recognized the existence of neutrons, they were able to calculate the binding energy or the amount of energy required to break the nucleus into its component parts, neutrons and protons. In addition, a neutron was large enough to knock out a proton from the nucleus of an atom. For experimental physicists all around the world, this discovery meant that they could design new and interesting research projects that used neutrons to explore what was happening inside an atom's nucleus.

When Irène and Frédéric conducted a series of experiments with the Wilson cloud chamber, they observed tiny electron-like particles behaving in unpredicted and unusual ways by curving in the opposite direction (which indicated a positive charge). They were "going backwards the wrong way," Frédéric reported. In other words, it appeared as if the tracks had been made by a positively charged particle, something scientists had not previously observed.

What was it? Irène and Frédéric considered two possible explanations: A wayward electron could have entered the airtight chamber inadvertently through the wall and headed straight for the neutrons, or they could have discovered a strange, new particle—a positron—a positively charged particle, or "anti-electron."

Again, the Joliot-Curies published their findings before they fully understood the significance of what they had seen.

Instead of recognizing that they had created evidence to support the existence of the position, Irène and Frédéric had left the question open for another researcher to correctly interpret. A few months later, Carl David Anderson of the United

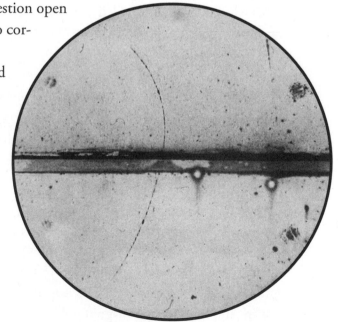

This image from a Wilson cloud chamber shows the first positron as observed by Carl David Anderson. When the Joliot-Curies reviewed their images, they found that they had also seen a positron, but they had misinterpreted their data.

States repeated the Joliot-Curies' experiment and discovered the positron. When Irène and Frédéric learned about Anderson's discovery, they looked back at their photographs and realized that they had also found evidence of positrons. It was too late now: Anderson earned the credit for identifying the positron and won the 1936 Nobel Prize in Physics.

Right on Time

In their next round of research, Irène and Frédéric continued to search for positrons. They designed an experiment in which they exposed both medium-weight and lightweight elements to radioactive polonium. They found that the medium-weight elements always released protons, but lightweight elements sometimes released a proton and other times released a combination of a neutron and a positron.

This was the research that they presented at the 1933 Solvay Conference. This was the research that their colleagues dismissed when Lise Meitner challenged their findings. Most importantly, this was the research that led Frédéric back to the laboratory on the night that the Joliot-Curies discovered artificial radioactivity. When he repeated the experiment with the Geiger counter next to the non-radioactive metal, he realized that the polonium had somehow transferred its radioactivity to the other metal. This time, the Joliot-Curies recognized the importance of their findings. Frédéric said: "With the neutron we were too late; with the positron we were too late—now we were on time."

The Nobel Prize in Chemistry, 1935

Throughout 1934, the Joliot-Curies continued their research on artificial radioactivity. Within months they had created radioactive nitrogen and boron, as well as isotopes of phosphorus from aluminum, and silicon from magnesium.

Irène and Frédéric were not nominated for the Nobel Prize in 1934—it often took time for the Nobel Committee to fully appreciate the significance of discoveries. But the following year, they received the telegram from Stockholm informing them that they had won the 1935 Nobel Prize in Chemistry. Their Nobel Prize brought Irène's family's total to five. (Years later, when Eve's husband, diplomat Henry R. Labouisse, accepted a Nobel Peace Prize for the United Nations Children's Emergency Fund in 1965, the total for the entire Curie family rose to six. Eve joked that she had brought shame on the family. She said: "I am the only one of the family not to have won a Nobel Prize. There were [six] Nobel Prizes in my family. Two for my mother, one for my father, one [each] for my sister and brother-in-law, and one for my husband. Only I was not successful.")

Irène Joliot-Curie's official photograph when she was awarded the Nobel Prize in Chemistry with Frédéric Joliot-Curie for the discovery of artificial radioactivity.

In accordance with custom, an afternoon tea was held in the garden at the Radium Institute in honor of the Joliot-Curies. When someone asked how she felt about receiving the Nobel Prize, Irène paused and said, "In our family, we are accustomed to glory."

This was the same attitude she had expressed years earlier when Frédéric asked her how she felt about living in a famous family. At first she didn't understand the question: *Famous family?* Then she

King Gustaf V of Sweden shaking hands with Irène Joliot-Curie, who shared the 1935 Nobel Prize in Chemistry with her husband, Frédéric, standing behind her.

said, "Fame was something from the outside. It really had no connection with us." They were merely scientists exploring the world around them.

All the same, Irène beamed with pride when her name was called and the king of Sweden presented her with a diploma and medal during the Nobel ceremony. No doubt Irène thought about her mother and father and their appearance on the same stage years before. Irène's enthusiasm didn't last all night, however. She soon became bored by the reception, and when King Gustav asked where she was, Frédéric found her in a corner, reading a book.

When they returned to Paris, Irène and Frédéric went back to their laboratory, refreshed and ready to continue their research. All around the world, researchers focused on the creating on new radioactive elements. Several teams of investigators shared this passion for the study of radioactivity, and one of their greatest rivals was Lise Meitner, the woman who had challenged the Joliot-Curies at the 1933 Solvay Conference.

LOST AND FOUND

Growing up, Lise Meitner did not enjoy the privileged status that Irène Curie did as the first-born child in the world's "First Family" of science. Instead, Meitner, born on November 7, 1878, was the third of eight children of Philipp Meitner, one of the first Jewish lawyers in Vienna, then the capital of the Austro-Hungarian Empire. Meitner wasn't German and she wasn't a practicing Jew—she grew up in an agnostic household and converted to Protestantism in 1908—but she became a victim of Adolf Hitler's Nazi Germany nonetheless.

The Meitner children were taught to be independent. Meitner's mother, Hedwig, told her children: "Listen to me and to your father but think for yourself!" They were encouraged to study science, and Meitner's mother, a talented pianist, gave her children music lessons. When opportunities in higher education were open to girls, the family encouraged all eight of the Meitner children—both girls and boys—to pursue advanced degrees. Not surprisingly, music and physics became Meitner's lifelong passions. Meitner's older sister, Auguste or Gusti, became a concert pianist; another sister, Frida, earned a doctorate in physics and became a college professor. One of her brothers, Walter, earned a Ph.D. in chemistry, and another, Fritz, became an engineer.

Meitner showed an early fascination with science. As a young child, she wondered why a puddle with a bit of oil on it showed lovely colors, and when someone explained that the oil rises to the top because oil is lighter than water and then it refracts the light like a rainbow, she was thrilled to discover "that there were such things to find out about our world." By the time she was eight years old, Meitner hid math books under her pillow and blocked the crack beneath her bedroom door at night so that her parents wouldn't stop her from studying past her bedtime.

Whenever she encountered an article or news account about Marie and Pierre Curie, Meitner paid special attention. About ten years younger than Marie Curie (and 20 years older than Irène), Meitner idolized the French physicists and imagined someday following a similar path in the sciences. Marie's work inspired Meitner to believe that a life in the sciences was possible for a woman.

As a teenager dreaming about her future, Meitner always made the same wish: "Life need not be easy, provided only that it is not empty." Her life proved to be neither easy nor empty.

The "Lost Years"

By age fourteen, Meitner had completed her basic education. She had learned enough arithmetic, geography, drawing, singing, French, and religion to be able to one day manage a household and raise children, so her formal education was over. In fact, Austrian law banned girls from attending gymnasiums, the academic high schools that prepared boys to attend universities. This makes the Meitner daughters' accomplishments all the more impressive.

Meitner called the years from 1892 to 1901 when she was denied an education her "lost years," and she believed that they handicapped her for life. She begged for an education—she desperately wanted to study physics—but there was nothing her parents could do to enroll her in school.

As a young woman, Meitner had no interest in marriage and children, and her father worried about how she would support herself without a husband. Her fantasy of becoming a physicist seemed particularly impractical because there were few jobs in the field for men, and none for women. There were very few jobs in industry for physicists, and universities considered physics a dead subject, on the grounds there was very little left to be learned about the physical world. In neighboring Germany in the late 19th century, the president of the National Bureau of Standards announced: "Nothing else has to be done in physics than just make better measurements." Little did he know that Marie Curie was about to make a series of discoveries that would revolutionize the understanding of the atom and all physical matter.

To ensure that Meitner could make a living, her father insisted that she spend three years earning a certificate that would qualify her to teach French at a girls' finishing school. In 1899, during Meitner's second year of the program, the Austrian government changed its approach to education and announced that universities would have to admit qualified women, even if they did not have a gymnasium degree. For the first time, girls would be allowed to sit for the university entrance tests, but they would still have to score high enough to be accepted. At the time, the knowledge required to pass the Matura test was nearly equivalent to a two-year college degree today.

After Meitner completed her French certificate, her father agreed to hire a private tutor to prepare her for the university entrance exams. In addition to the science courses, Meitner was drilled for exams in mathematics, physics, psychology, German literature, Greek, Latin, and French, zoology, botany, mineralogy, logic, history, and religion. In two years, Meitner completed eight years' worth of schoolwork, including eight years of Latin and six years of Greek.

Whenever she took a break from her work, her younger brothers and sisters teased her: "Lise, you're going to flunk. You have just walked through the room without studying!"

In the end, Meitner's steady work paid off. Of the 14 women who took the university entrance examination with Meitner, only four passed, and one of them was Meitner. Meitner enrolled at the University of Vienna in October 1901, just a few months short of her 23rd birthday. Meitner's "lost years" were over.

To the "Henhouse"

Meitner was the first woman admitted to the University of Vienna's physics department. In her enthusiasm, she enrolled in a heavy course load: twenty-five hours a week of calculus, physics, chemistry,

The University of Vienna, Austria-Hungary, as it appeared around 1900.

and botany. Her work was so difficult and time-consuming that she often had to study late into the night, and then she struggled to stay awake in class during the day. Although she enjoyed all of her coursework, by the second half of her first year she decided to concentrate on physics, which included the study of matter, magnetism, heat, light, sound, and electricity.

At that time, female university students were widely thought of as misfits. Some men welcomed and supported women pursuing higher education, but others did their best to make the female students feel that they did not belong. For the most part, Meitner kept to herself. She was extremely shy, and she didn't worry much about how she got along with the other students. In her free time, she enjoyed attending concerts either alone or with a few friends. She bought the cheapest seats in the Vienna opera house, high up under the ceiling, an area she called her "musical heaven." She brought her own musical scores to many concerts and read the music as she listened to the performances.

Four years later, Meitner had completed her coursework and began work on her doctoral thesis, involving the way heat is conducted through solids. In February 1906, she graduated *summa cum laude*, with highest honors, with a doctoral degree in physics. The 27-year-old was only the second woman to earn a doctorate in physics in the university's 500-year history.

Even with a doctorate in physics, it was difficult for Meitner to find work. At the time, most Austrian physicists worked at universities, beginning in a position called Assistant, but there had never been a female assistant in Austria. After being turned down in the world of academia—and to please her father—she spent the next year teaching French at a girls' high school.

Meitner didn't give up on her dream, however. In addition to teaching, she helped English physicist Lord Rayleigh translate his scientific papers on optics from English to German. She also helped Rayleigh prove a point about optical reflection that he had been

Lise Meitner at the time she was a doctoral student at the University of Vienna in 1906.

struggling with. Based on this experience, she went on to publish her first postdoctoral research papers. She also conducted studies on the effects of alpha particles passing through various types of matter. (In order to perform her experiment, she used a piece of radium that had been donated to the University of Vienna by Marie and Pierre Curie in appreciation for Austria-Hungary's gift of the minerals Marie used in her research.)

In her spare time, Meitner continued to study, and she worked without pay at the Institute for Theoretical Physics, the laboratory at the university referred to as the "henhouse" because of its disheveled appearance. She developed a serious interest in radioactivity and applied for full-time work at Marie Curie's Radium Institute in Paris. Curie turned her down.

Undaunted, Meitner continued with her work. In 1906, the university administration invited the famous physicist Max Planck to consider a post as a visiting professor. Planck decided to remain in Berlin, but Meitner had been impressed with him and his work, so she applied for post-doctoral study at the University of Berlin and was accepted.

At the time, Germany was considered the scientific center of the world. The country had transformed itself into a great, technologically advanced power by investing in universities and technical schools. Berlin was home to famous Nobel Prize–winning physicists like Planck, Albert Einstein, and Max von Laue. Planck was developing his quantum theory, which postulated that atoms absorb and release energy in little packets called quanta. (In 1918 Planck would win the Nobel Prize in Physics for this work.)

Meitner's determination and hard work had impressed her father so much that he agreed to give her an allowance to study in Berlin for one semester. She expected to stay there for about six months—maybe a year—but she had no idea how exciting the world of physics was about to become.

Off to Berlin

In the fall of 1907 at age 28, Meitner moved to Berlin, which had become a gathering place for talented young physicists. Prussian universities did not give women credit toward university degrees at the time, but Meitner was permitted to audit classes. When Meitner arrived at the University of Berlin, she introduced herself to Planck and asked for permission to take his classes. Meitner recalled their first meeting:

> When I registered with Planck at the University of Berlin in order to attend his lectures, he received me very kindly and soon afterward invited me to his home. The first time I visited him there, he said to me, "But you are a Doctor already! What more do you want?" When I replied that I would like to gain some real understanding of physics, he just said a few friendly words and did not pursue the matter any further.

Planck did not approve of women students. In response to an 1897 questionnaire of 104 university professors about the "women's issue," Planck had responded:

If a woman has a special gift for the tasks of theoretical physics, which does not happen often but it happens sometimes, and moreover she herself feels moved to develop her gift, I do not think it right, both personally and impersonally, to refuse her the chance and means of studying for reasons of principle. . . . On the other hand, I must keep to the fact that such a case must always be regarded just as an *exception*.

Planck's initial reaction to Meitner was typical of German professors of his generation. Three German words—*Kinder, Küche, Kirche*; children, kitchen, church—summed up the acceptable roles of women in Germany at that time. Official German policy still barred women from taking classes as full-time students, regardless of their citizenship or academic achievements. (At the University of Berlin, women would not be allowed to attend classes full-time until 1909, two years after Meitner arrived.) Meitner was in Berlin to learn whatever she could from the experts in her field; she didn't like it, but she was willing to tolerate being treated as inferior to men in order to benefit from the experiences she could have. It was a fascinating time to be studying physics.

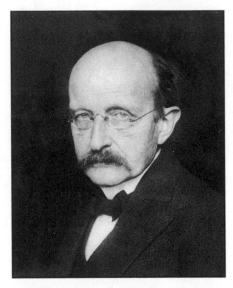

Max Planck, 1933. Planck (1858–1947) was a German physicist best known for developing quantum theory. He won the Nobel Prize in Physics in 1918.

Meitner was impressed with Planck's quantum theory, and she thought it offered great possibilities for understanding the nature of matter. Once she got to know Planck, she admired him greatly. He had "a rare honesty of mind and an almost naïve straightforwardness," she said. In Berlin she was doing what she loved—at last.

Partnering with Hahn

When not attending Planck's lectures, Meitner wanted to design and conduct experiments involving radioactivity, but she needed access to a laboratory. First, she approached Heinrich Rubens, the head of the University of Berlin's department of experimental physics, to ask if she could use a laboratory there to do her research. He told her that the only space he had was in his laboratory, working under him.

While she appreciated his offer, she wanted to do independent research. She was trying to figure out how to turn down his offer without offending him, when he mentioned that a young physicist named Otto Hahn was looking for a physicist to help him with radiation experiments. Hahn himself came in a few minutes later. As Meitner later recalled:

> Hahn was of the same age as myself and very informal in manner, and I had a feeling that I would have no hesitation in asking him all I needed to know. Moreover, he had a very good reputation in the field of radioactivity, so I was convinced that he could teach me a great deal.

In addition, Hahn was charming, and his outgoing personality compensated for Meitner's shyness.

Meitner, a physicist, and Hahn, a chemist, began a partnership and friendship that would last more than 30 years and span two world wars. In many ways, they made an odd couple: She was slender and petite; he was sturdy and tall. She was shy; he was outgoing. She had a subtle, sophisticated sense of humor; he was a joker. She was a critical thinker who reasoned systematically; he was intuitive and did things without always knowing exactly why. What they shared was curiosity and a love of science.

After they decided to work together, they encountered problems because Meitner was a woman. Hahn worked at Emil Fischer's Institute of Chemistry in Berlin, and Fischer did not allow women in his laboratories. He said that he banned women because he worried that their hair would catch fire on the Bunsen burners, but he allowed men with facial hair and long beards to work in the lab. Hahn urged Fischer to reconsider, and he eventually agreed to allow Meitner to work with Hahn if she promised not to go upstairs into the main chemistry department. Instead, she had to work in a small room in the basement that originally had been planned as a carpenter's workshop. (If Meitner had to use the bathroom, she had to walk down the street to a hotel with a women's room.)

Meitner was thrilled to have a place to work. She would meet Hahn in the afternoons, after Hahn had spent the day working at the Institute and Meitner had attended lectures at the university. They often worked into the evening, hours after everyone else had gone home. They kept their friendship very formal: Hahn called Meitner "Fräulein Meitner" and she called him "Herr Hahn" for many years. Despite the formality, the two got along very well. Meitner wrote about her experiences working with Hahn:

> When I think back on our more than 30-year collaboration, apart from the scientific experiences, my strongest and dearest remembrances are of Hahn's almost indestructible cheerfulness and serene disposition, his constant helpfulness and his joy in music. Although he doesn't play an instrument, he is markedly gifted musically, with a very good musical ear and an extraordinarily good musical memory. I remember he was given to singing or whistling the themes of all the movements of the complete Beethoven symphonies and some of the themes from Tchaikovsky's symphonies. If he was in an especially good mood, he would whistle large parts of Beethoven's violin concerto and would sometimes purposely

change the rhythm of the last movement, only to laugh about my protest to it. When we worked in the woodworking shop (we still had no assistants) we would frequently sing Brahms duets, particularly when the work went well.

And the work was going well much of the time.

At first, Meitner and Hahn studied beta radiation, measuring radiation from every known element. (Beta particles are electrons or positrons ejected from the nuclei of radioactive atoms.) They published three articles in 1908 and six more in 1909. This was a very productive time for them as they developed a basic understanding of radioactivity, and they also learned how to work together as research partners.

In a Man's World

In 1909, two years after Meitner began working in the basement laboratory, Prussia opened its universities to women. At that point, Fischer allowed Meitner to enter the rest of the building and visit the upstairs labs for the first time. (He even installed a toilet for her.) He recognized Meitner's brilliance and her impeccable work ethic, and he became one of her strongest supporters.

Other men in the laboratory, however, never got used to the idea of having a woman in the lab. When Meitner and Hahn walked together in the street, Fischer's young male assistants greeted him with "Good day, Herr Hahn," intentionally ignoring Meitner. She never responded to the insults.

Meitner also encountered prejudice from men in other related fields. An encyclopedia editor liked one of her articles so much that he asked "Herr Meitner" to write more. When he learned that "Herr Meitner" was actually "Fraülein Meitner," the editor wrote back to say that he would not dream of publishing anything written by a woman!

Sometimes scientists in other labs did not realize Meitner was a woman. When Ernest Rutherford, a physicist from New Zealand, visited Berlin, Hahn brought him to Meitner's downstairs laboratory to meet her. When he shook her hand, Rutherford said: "Oh, I thought you were a man!" Meitner found the remark amusing. Her only frustration came later when the men stayed behind to discuss their research on radioactivity and she was expected to take Mrs. Rutherford out Christmas shopping.

Meitner was always very generous about giving Hahn credit for work that she could have published on her own. Working by herself, Meitner discovered that radioactive thorium decayed into a substance she called "thorium D." A well-known professional recommended that she publish the results by herself and Hahn agreed, but she submitted the article as a team with both their names anyway. "He was much better known than I," she later explained.

In the early years, when it came time for them to announce their research findings, Meitner always insisted that Hahn present their work. She was shy and an inexperienced speaker. They were the same age, but because of her educational delay, Hahn had considerably more professional experience and confidence.

Sometimes friends asked why Meitner and Hahn did not marry each other. When asked, Meitner said: "Oh, my dear, I just didn't have enough time for that!" Hahn explained:

> There was no question of any closer relationship between us outside the laboratory. Lise Meitner had had a strict, ladylike upbringing and was very reserved, even shy. I used to lunch with my colleague Franz Fischer almost every day and go to the café with him on Wednesdays, but for many years I never had a meal with Lise Meitner except on official occasions. Nor did we ever go for a walk together. Apart from the physics colloquia that we attended, we met only in the carpenter's shop. There we generally worked until nearly

eight in the evening . . . One or the other of us would have to go out to buy salami or cheese before the shops shut at that hour. We never ate our cold supper together there. Lise Meitner went home alone, and so did I. And yet we were really very close friends.

The work Meitner did with Hahn was unpaid, yet as long as she was working in a lab, Meitner was unlikely to find a husband willing and able to offer her financial support. Instead, she continued to rely on an allowance from her father as her sole source of income.

Though Meitner never married, she had a number of close friendships that endured her entire life. She was a devoted and loyal friend, who found the most significant meaning and satisfaction in her work. This period of intellectual and creative freedom brought her joy and genuine personal fulfillment.

A LAB OF HER OWN

URING HER TIME in Berlin, Lise Meitner thrived both professionally and personally. In the laboratory, Meitner earned a reputation as a stern and somewhat aloof leader. She was known to be a careful and creative researcher.

While some of the men Meitner worked with in the lab shunned her and tried to make her uncomfortable, some of the world's most accomplished scientists, including Max Planck, Albert Einstein, James Franck, Niels Bohr, Max Born, Erwin Schrödinger, and Max von Laue, respected her as a colleague and friend. "They were also exceptionally nice people to know," Meitner explained. "Each was ready to help the other; each welcomed the other's success. You can understand what it meant to me to be received in such a friendly manner into this circle."

Wednesday Colloquia

"Radioactivity and atomic physics were making unbelievably fast progress," Meitner said. "Nearly every month there was a wonderful, surprising new discovery in one of the laboratories working in these areas." To keep up with the rapidly evolving research, Heinrich Rubens started to hold weekly colloquia, or seminars, for physicists to explain their work. Every Wednesday, Meitner and several dozen other physicists from Berlin's various research institutes gathered to listen to a lecture. This allowed them to learn about work that was being done in all areas of physics. The front bench was famous: It was composed almost entirely of Nobel Prize winners, plus Meitner.

"That colloquium was the greatest event in my life," said James Franck, who won the Nobel Prize in Physics in 1925 for his work on atomic structure. "We could see how the great men of that time had all struggled with their problems. . . . The reason that many of us . . . tried to do something with quantum theory is that we went to that colloquium." Meitner said:

> By 1907 these colloquia were already an exceptional center of intellectual activity. All the new results that were then pour-ing out were presented and discussed. I remember lectures on astronomy, physics, chemistry—for example, a lecture on the stars of various ages given by [Karl] Schwarzschild, a theoreti-cal astronomer; another by James Franck on what were then called metastable states of atoms, or one on the connection between ionization energy and quantum theory. It was quite extraordinary what one could acquire there in the way of knowledge and learning.

The development of physics became, she said, "A magic, musical ac-companiment to my life."

Some lectures had a lasting and significant impact on Meitner's thinking. For example, Meitner distinctly remembered when she heard Albert Einstein speak at a conference in Salzburg. More than fifty years later, she recalled:

> At that time I did not yet realize the full implications of
> the theory of relativity and they way in which it would

contribute to a revolutionary transformation of our concepts of time and space. In the course of this lecture, [Einstein] did, however, take the theory of relativity and from it derive the equation: energy equals mass times the square of the velocity of light [$E=mc^2$], and showed that to every radiation must be attributed an inert mass. These two facts were so overwhelmingly new and surprising that, to this day, I remember the lecture very well.

While she didn't understand its significance at the moment, she remembered the details of this lecture years later and drew on it when she had an epiphany about nuclear fission.

The Kaiser Wilhelm Institutes

In 1912, the German government set up a network of independent, state-of-the-art academic research laboratories that had been founded and funded by private companies. The Kaiser Wilhelm Society was an umbrella group that oversaw three large institutes located about fifteen miles outside of Berlin, specializing in chemistry, physical chemistry, and biochemistry.

When the Kaiser Wilhelm Institutes opened, Otto Hahn accepted a position as head of the radiochemistry section of the Chemistry Institute with a salary of 5,000 marks a year. At the same time, Meitner was invited to work in Hahn's lab as an unpaid "guest." Meitner desperately wanted to work with Hahn at the Institute, but money had become a problem. Her father had died about a year before, so she no longer had his financial support. She made some money translating scientific articles from English to German and writing articles for popular science journals, but not enough to support herself.

At that time, the University of Prague offered Meitner a post as an associate professor; she didn't want to leave Germany, but

The Kaiser Wilhelm Institutes were founded in 1911 to promote the natural sciences in Germany by creating research institutes independent of the state. That said, they were put in service to the military for weapons development during both world wars.

she couldn't afford to stay if she couldn't earn a salary. Meitner told Planck that she had no choice but to accept the paid position, and he responded by asking her to become his assistant at the university. In 1912, five years after arriving in Berlin, Meitner became Prussia's first female research assistant, grading class assignments for 200 students and organizing Planck's seminars. Meitner was thrilled. She said:

> Not only did this give me a chance to work under such a wonderful man and eminent scientist as Planck, it was also the entrance to my scientific career. It was the passport to scientific activity in the eyes of most scientists and a great help in overcoming many current prejudices against academic women.

The salary wasn't generous, but it was enough for her to remain in Berlin and continue the work she loved.

Meitner split her time between her work at the university and her research at the Chemistry Institute. She worked with Hahn on various studies of radioactivity, but their work slowed when the country went to war in 1914.

Meitner During the War

In the early months of World War I, Meitner learned about the work Marie and Irène Curie were doing with X-rays for military hospitals. Inspired by the Curies' use of X-rays, Meitner considered the possibility of doing similar work in Austria—but for the German side rather than the French.

Since the war had started, the German scientific community had fallen into chaos. Students and scientists had left their laboratories and lecture halls to fight for Germany, and the military had converted classrooms and warehouses into hospitals and mobilization centers. Otto Hahn had been drafted to work on a chemical weapons project. Meitner could not continue with her work as usual.

To support her homeland during the war, Meitner worked at the city hospital in Lichterfelde, outside Berlin. She took classes in human anatomy and X-ray technology, and in July 1915, Meitner returned to Vienna and volunteered as an X-ray technician and surgical nurse with the Austrian army. Within days she was trained, vaccinated, and assigned to a military hospital in Lemberg (now Lviv, Ukraine), not far from the Russian front. She was astonished at what she saw there. In early August she wrote to a friend:

> We are converting the local Technical Institute into a barracks hospital. Until now there was a field hospital here, with about 6,000 to 7,000 wounded who had to be transferred elsewhere as quickly as possible. Now as a barracks hospital at least some of the wounded can stay longer to make a recovery. . . . I never expected it to be as awful as it actually

Lise Meitner and Otto Hahn worked together in 1913 at a laboratory at the Kaiser Wilhelm Institute for Chemistry.

is. These poor people, who at best will be cripples, have the most horrible pains. One can hear their screams and groans as well as see their horrible wounds. Today we had a Czech who was severely wounded in his arms and legs who moaned in pain while tears ran down his face. . . . Since we are only about 40 km [25 miles] from the front we get only the most severely wounded here. I tell myself this for consolation. But one has one's own thoughts about war when one sees all this.

Meitner worked grueling hours, sometimes enduring 20-hour shifts when she was needed. The horrors she witnessed taught her to hate war. On October 14, 1915, Meitner wrote to Hahn:

> You can hardly imagine my way of life. That there is physics, that I used to work in physics, and that I will again, seems much out of reach as if it had never happened and never will again in the future. At night, in bed, when I cannot immediately fall asleep, sometimes homesick thoughts come to me. During the day, I think only about my patients.
>
> I have completed over 200 X-ray films, but that still leaves me much time to help in the surgery room. . . . The gratitude these people feel and show always makes me feel a little ashamed. Often time these people suffer so terribly and cannot be helped at all.

Hahn well understood the agonies of war. He had been assigned to do chemical research as part of the German Gas Warfare Corps in Wittenberg, Germany, but he was initially unaware that the noxious substances he was creating were to be used against soldiers. When he learned the truth, Hahn said he was profoundly ashamed and upset. He argued that using chemical weapons violated the Hague Convention, but he was told that in the end more lives would be saved than lost by using the toxic gas. Hahn did not press the issue further. On April 22, 1915, Germany released 168 tons of chlorine gas over French lines in Ypres, Belgium, in the world's first poison-gas attack.

In addition to spending time in the laboratory, Hahn was sent into the trenches near Belgium to serve in combat with the 126th Infantry Regiment. Forty years after the war, a German journalist interviewed Hahn and asked about his experience during World War I. Hahn said:

> First, we attacked the Russian soldiers with our gases, and then when we saw the poor fellows lying there, dying

slowly, we tried to make breathing easier for them by using life-saving devices on them. It made us realize that utter
senselessness of war. First you do your utmost to finish off
the stranger over there in the enemy trench, and then when
you're face to face with him, you can't bear the sight of what
you've done and you try to help him. But we couldn't save
the poor fellows.

Hahn felt that he had no alternative but to do as he was instructed.
Years later, Hahn wrote in his memoirs: "As a result of continuous
work with these highly toxic gases, our minds were so numbed that
we no longer had any scruples about the whole thing."

The German chemical weapons program had been directed by
Fritz Haber, a Jewish chemist who argued in favor of the use of gas:
"It was a way of saving countless lives, if it meant that the war could
be brought to an end sooner." Haber's wife, also a chemist, begged
her husband to stop creating and using poison gas. He refused to listen; in desperation, she committed suicide by shooting herself in the
heart with his service revolver on the night he returned to the front
to orchestrate additional gas attacks.

Toxic gases similar to those formulated by Haber would be used
against the Jews during World War II.

Discovering Protactinium

Meitner's scientific work continued during the war years as well.
Before leaving for her war service, Meitner had set up a long-term
experiment at the Kaiser Wilhelm Institute designed to establish the
link between the radioactive elements uranium (atomic number 92)
and actinium (atomic number 89). Whenever she had time off or a
leave of absence, Meitner returned to her lab to monitor the project.

When Hahn told Meitner that her laboratory was going to
be taken over for military research, she was distraught. If soldiers

disrupted her workspace, her experiments in progress would be destroyed and years of work would be lost. In the fall of 1917, Meitner resigned from her military service and returned full-time to her laboratory at the Kaiser Wilhelm Institute. Her diligent effort to keep her multi-year experiment from being interrupted ultimately paid off: She detected alpha radiation coming from the sample in her experiment, then she identified that it contained actinium, just as she had predicted in her first hypothesis. She then boiled the sample in acid, filtered the remains, and dried the solid precipitate formed during the chemical reaction. She repeated the process with a stronger acid, further purifying the substance. After several months of systematic work, Meitner had isolated a new element—the precursor to actinium—and she named it protactinium (atomic number 91). Her experiment established that actinium is a product of the radioactive decay of protactinium.

On March 16, 1918, Meitner and Hahn published a paper titled "The Mother Substance of Actinium, a New Radioactive Element of Long Half-Life" in the *Journal of Physical Chemistry*. Even though Hahn did not assist with much of the research, Meitner insisted on giving him credit for his early contribution to the work. She even listed his name first on the paper, later saying that she did so because he was better known than she was.

Postwar Opportunities

World War I ended on November 11, 1918, when Germany surrendered. By the end of the war, Meitner had established herself as one of the world's leading physicists, and she was ready to find out if the postwar world was a better place for a woman scientist to work. Although Germany experienced economic hardship after the war, the Institute continued to flourish because the Germans wanted to use it to improve their industries and help get the country back on its feet. IG Farben, a German chemical company that had supported the Institute during the last years of the war, continued to finance the research facility.

Meitner was asked to organize a new physics department at the Chemistry Institute, and she became its director. She was also given the resources to develop an experimental physics lab that rivaled the Curies' Radium Institute in Paris or Rutherford's Cavendish Laboratory in Cambridge, England.

In 1921, Meitner began teaching in the physics department at the University of Berlin, and she became an assistant professor four years later. In spite of her past achievements and reputation, she had to pass an oral examination and present a public lecture to demonstrate her thorough knowledge of physics. She had become interested in radiation studies in astrophysics, so she prepared her inaugural talk on "The Significance of Radioactivity for Cosmic Processes." The academic press in Berlin published a notice about Meitner's lecture—the first by a woman—but they reported the topic as "The Significant of Radioactivity for Cosmetic Processes."

Meitner thrived in the position and in 1926, at age 47, she became Germany's first female full professor of physics. The years between 1926 and 1938 were among the most productive and happiest for Meitner. She excelled in her work and established a reputation as one of the

A portrait of Lise Meitner taken in the 1930s, during one of the most productive and satisfying periods of her career.

world's finest physicists. Einstein called her "our German Madame Curie."

While great strides were made in understanding the atom at that time, the potential significance of atomic power was not always well understood. In 1933, Einstein told a reporter that the attempts at "loosening the energy of the atom were fruitless." The same year, physicist Ernest Rutherford also said, "Anyone who expects a source of power from the transformation of atoms is talking moonshine." No one had a clear appreciation of the many ways in which the world was about to change.

Despite all that she had witnessed during the war, Meitner remained idealistic about the role physics could play in the world. She still believed her work would positively influence people for many generations. She wrote to a friend, "I love physics with all my heart. I can hardly imagine it not being a part of my life. It is a kind of personal love, as one has for a person to whom one is grateful for many things."

8

RADIUM: TREATMENT OR TOXIN?

LISE MEITNER AND Irène Curie may have had lofty and benevolent ideas about how physics could be used for the benefit of mankind, but not everyone shared their opinions. Some corporations saw an opportunity to use the new breakthroughs in science as a way to make money.

In the 1920s and 1930s, radium was promoted as a miracle drug. Doctors prescribed medications and procedures that used radioactive elements in the treatment of cancer—just as they do today—but they also relied on it to treat gout, arthritis, dermatitis, some forms of tuberculosis, and other conditions.

During World War I, medics gave intravenous injections of radium solutions to soldiers who suffered from severe blood loss, and they used external treatments of radium to stimulate nerves, loosen joints, and relax scar tissue.

Manufacturers and marketers soon began using radioactivity to promote their commercial products. Want a sparkling smile? Brush with radium toothpaste! How about a glowing complexion? Try radium-infused skin creams! Need a pick-me-up? Soak in radioactive bath salts! By 1929, there were at least eighty patent medicines containing radioactive ingredients sold in Europe, and many in the United States as well. Radium was added to cosmetics, chocolates, and cigarettes, among other products, along with the claim that these enhanced products would support longevity, virility, and overall good health.

Advertisers were not above using the Curie name to shill products. Irène and her mother consulted an attorney in attempt to stop an advertising campaign that used "Dr. Alfred Curie" to sell Tho-Radia face powder. It turned out that there was a real French doctor named Alfred Curie—no relation to Marie and Pierre—and he sold an entire line of radioactive beauty products that contained the active ingredients thorium chloride and radium bromide, both radioactive.

A container of Dr. Alfred Curie's Tho-Radia powder, on display at the Curie Museum in Paris.

It was not long before evidence surfaced that many of these products and treatments were outright dangerous and potentially deadly. Both patients receiving treatment and the doctors administering them began to experience symptoms ranging from radio-dermatitis (skin irritation caused by exposure to radiation) to radium necrosis (tissue death resulting in gangrene and sometimes death). People gradually began to realize that too much radiation was harmful, but no one knew how much was too much.

The "Undark" Dial Painters

Probably the most well-known cases of radium poisoning took place in the 1920s in Orange, New Jersey. The United States Radium Corporation hired hundreds of young women to paint watchdial numerals and instrument dials with Undark brand paint, a glow-in-the-dark formula that contained trace amounts of radium. To paint the thin lines, the women used ultra-fine brushes made up of just a few camel hairs. To keep the points sharp, the women were encouraged to twirl the brush tips between their lips, often swallowing small amounts of the paint in the process.

At the time, no one thought the practice presented any health risks. The paint contained tiny amounts of radium: one part radium to thirty thousand or more parts of zinc sulfide. Not only were these doses small enough to be assumed harmless, but at that time, many people actually thought the radium exposure offered health benefits. In truth, the women working for U.S. Radium were being poisoned with each of the 250 dials they painted every day.

In the body, radium replaces calcium in the bones. Over time radium exposure causes bones to deteriorate, resulting in decomposing jaws, bleeding gums, severe anemia, weakness, and cancer of the bones and bone marrow. Women at the U.S. Radium plant began showing symptoms of radium poisoning, and in 1925, five of them sued their employer. Three years later, they won their case—a

A 1921 magazine advertisement for Undark, a product of the Radium Luminous Material Corporation.

landmark victory for worker's rights—but by that time more than fifteen workers had died.

After the lawsuit, an American journalist asked Marie Curie what advice she would offer the dial painters. She encouraged them to eat calves' liver for iron and to exercise in the fresh air. That was her universal remedy for radiation-related sickness.

"Dangerous to the Health"

Evidence continued to mount that radiation could cause serious health problems. In France, several deaths were associated with exposure to radioactive materials, including an acquaintance of Irène's who worked with mesothorium and radium and died after spilling radioactive materials on herself. In a separate incident, two engineers died of leukemia and anemia after preparing radioactive materials for medical use.

At the Radium Institute where Irène worked, Sonia Cotelle, a Polish chemist and longtime worker at the laboratory, had an accident in which polonium exploded in her face. Irène wrote to Marie, reporting that Cotelle was "in very bad health . . . she has stomach troubles, an extremely rapid loss of hair, etc.," and suggested that she may have swallowed some of the radioactive element. Another one of Irène's coworkers experienced serious vision problems, and there were cases of radiodermatitis that had ultimately resulted in the loss of fingers. There were other deaths in the laboratory: one man who died of bronchitis and two who died of tuberculosis. In hindsight, they seem tragic and likely caused or worsened by exposure to radioactivity.

In response to this cluster of deaths, in 1925 the French Academy of Medicine appointed a commission—headed by Marie Curie—to investigate the safety of those who worked with radioactive materials. Four years earlier, the Academy had prepared a similar report that concluded that the public had "unjustified fears" about the use of radioactive materials. This time, Marie and the other authors of the report took a different position.

The 1925 commission praised the 1921 report, but acknowledged the danger of handling radioactive materials—especially radium and thorium—without appropriate safety precautions. The report also warned against the inhalation of alpha particles, which could cause changes in the blood. The report offered several safety recommendations, including enclosing radioactive materials in heavy metal, using a one-inch-thick lead screen to separate workers from the radioactive source, and requiring that people who work with radioactive materials have their blood tested periodically to look for abnormalities. Finally, the report recommended that "industrial establishments which prepare, manipulate, or transport radioactive bodies be classified as dangerous to the health" and that they be regulated by the Ministry of Work and Health.

As a member of the commission, Marie was not recommending any practices that her laboratory did not already have in place. While she and Irène were often cavalier about radium burns and exposure to radiation for themselves, the Radium Institute did attempt to protect its workers in accordance with the standards of the day. As early as 1921, workers at the Radium Institute had policies in place requiring routine blood tests, safe storage of radioactive substances, use of protective lead screens, and use of forceps rather than their fingers when holding radioactive vials.

Rather than reassuring workers of their safety, blood tests at the Radium Institute showed that workers were exposed to unsafe levels of radiation in spite of the precautions taken. In 1931, for example, seven out of twenty workers had anomalies in their blood. Those showing signs of blood disorders were sent to the country for fresh air and vacation. In fact, doctors believed that problems with radiation poisoning were temporary, and that rest and time outdoors could undo the damage. When Irène's blood count was abnormal

Irène and Frédéric Joliot-Curie skiing with a friend in the Alps in 1930. Marie Curie recommended outdoor exercise for those suffering from radiation exposure.

in 1927, Marie wrote to her brother: "Irène doesn't feel well yet. . . . She will be leaving soon for two weeks of winter sports and hopes that this stay in the mountains will be good for her anemia."

At that time, there were few public protections in place. As in Europe, radium-laced products were for sale in America in the first part of the 20th century. In the 1920s and 1930s, well-intentioned doctors sometimes prescribed "fortified" radioactive water to their patients to improve their health. In 1932, an American golfer named Eben Byers died after following his doctor's advice. After Byers injured his arm, his doctor told him to drink Radiothor, a patented, energy-boosting drink made of distilled water enhanced with traces of radium and mesothorium. It promised to eliminate fatigue, muscles aches, and joint pain, among other symptoms.

For five years, Byers drank several bottles of Radiothor a day. Eventually his jaw disintegrated, his teeth fell out, and his weight dropped below 100 pounds. He died at age 51; the autopsy report confirmed the cause of death was radium poisoning (however, it was actually due to cancers caused by radiation). His gruesome death received a lot of public attention, and in response, legislators passed regulations that limited the use of radioactive elements in consumer products. Irène did not take a public position on the use of radium in household products; she and other researchers still did not fully understand the health risks associated with exposure to radiation.

Lise's Laboratory

When Lise Meitner and Otto Hahn opened their new lab at the Kaiser Wilhelm Institute after World War I, they took special precautions to avoid radiation exposure. In their old lab, they sometimes had difficulty measuring radiation because their work space had been contaminated with trace amounts of radioactive materials. Meitner knew that a cleaner lab meant more reliable results, so she went to great lengths to keep the new facility scrupulously clean and free of radioactive contamination.

The facility was designed with hygiene and safety in mind. Meitner hung rolls of toilet paper next to telephone and door handles so they could be wiped clean. As a matter of policy, no one in the lab was allowed to shake hands. The library and other meeting spaces had dark and light chairs so that people who handled radioactive materials could sit only in designated areas. Her efforts paid off: 25 years later, the lab remained free of contamination.

More importantly, Meitner and Hahn did not suffer any known side effects associated with radiation exposure, even though they spent their careers working with radioactive elements. Both researchers lived long and healthy lives, well into their 80s.

Radium Takes Its Toll

Over the years, the Curies—Marie, Pierre, Irène, and Frédéric—had to have known that their beloved radium and polonium were having a negative impact on their health. They all suffered from the ill effects of radium poisoning, and all but Pierre died prematurely as a result of overexposure to radioactivity.

In hindsight, recognizing the damage done by radioactivity was not as obvious as it might seem. Radioactivity damages the body silently and invisibly, and it was not always apparent which health problems should be directly attributed to radiation exposure. There had never been a poison quite like it: an unseen agent that damaged the body over the course of many years, affecting different people in different ways. In addition, although radioactive materials could both heal and destroy, people preferred to see the virtues of radioactivity—its cancer-killing properties, rather than its cancer-causing effects.

Throughout her adult life, Irène suffered from intermittent health problems, including tuberculosis and radiation poisoning, but she refused to acknowledge these illnesses. Like her mother, she had a strong work ethic and she defined herself through her research. She did not want to admit that exposure to radiation had compromised her health because that would mean that she should give up what she loved most: her work.

9

HEAVY METALS

AS PHYSICISTS LEARNED more about atomic structure in the 1930s, they became increasingly curious about the possibility of making new elements. Over the years, scientists had painstakingly worked out a periodic table showing the position of all the known elements ranked by atomic number, or the number of protons in the atom's nucleus. Hydrogen ranks lowest with atomic number 1; uranium ranks highest of the naturally occurring elements at 92.

Scientists wanted to test the boundaries of physics as they knew it by creating new elements that did not exist in the natural world. Researchers hoped to create so-called "transuranic" elements—elements with atomic number higher than uranium's 92—by bombarding uranium with extra neutrons. They theorized that if a neutron could insert itself into a uranium nucleus, then the atom would give off a beta particle (a high-speed electron or positron) and the neutron would become a proton, creating a new element with an atomic number of 93 or higher.

The challenge captivated the imaginations of researchers around the world as teams of scientists competed against one another to be the first to create transuranic elements. Scientists engaged in

THE PERIODIC TABLE OF ELEMENTS

The periodic table provides a format for organizing the chemical elements based on their atomic number (the number of protons in the nucleus). The period of an element on the table indicates recurring patterns, which helps chemists analyze and anticipate chemical behavior. The first periodic table was designed in 1869 by Russian chemist Dmitri Mendeleev. The modern periodic table includes elements with atomic numbers from 1 (hydrogen) to 118 (ununoctium), although a few of the elements have not yet been confirmed.

Group→ ↓Period	1	2	3	4	5	6	7	8	9	10	11	12	13	14	15	16	17	18
1	1 H																	2 He
2	3 Li	4 Be											5 B	6 C	7 N	8 O	9 F	10 Ne
3	11 Na	12 Mg											13 Al	14 Si	15 P	16 S	17 Cl	18 Ar
4	19 K	20 Ca	21 Sc	22 Ti	23 V	24 Cr	25 Mn	26 Fe	27 Co	28 Ni	29 Cu	30 Zn	31 Ga	32 Ge	33 As	34 Se	35 Br	36 Kr
5	37 Rb	38 Sr	39 Y	40 Zr	41 Nb	42 Mo	43 Tc	44 Ru	45 Rh	46 Pd	47 Ag	48 Cd	49 In	50 Sn	51 Sb	52 Te	53 I	54 Xe
6	55 Cs	56 Ba	*	72 Hf	73 Ta	74 W	75 Re	76 Os	77 Ir	78 Pt	79 Au	80 Hg	81 Tl	82 Pb	83 Bi	84 Po	85 At	86 Rn
7	87 Fr	88 Ra	**	104 Rf	105 Db	106 Sg	107 Bh	108 Hs	109 Mt	110 Ds	111 Rg	112 Cn	113 Uut	114 Fl	115 Uup	116 Lv	117 Uus	118 Uuo

*	57 La	58 Ce	59 Pr	60 Nd	61 Pm	62 Sm	63 Eu	64 Gd	65 Tb	66 Dy	67 Ho	68 Er	69 Tm	70 Yb	71 Lu
**	89 Ac	90 Th	91 Pa	92 U	93 Np	94 Pu	95 Am	96 Cm	97 Bk	98 Cf	99 Es	100 Fm	101 Md	102 No	103 Lr

transuranic research were the same as those involved in analyzing the structure of the atom, including Irène Curie in France, Lise Meitner and Otto Hahn in Germany, Ernest Rutherford in Great Britain, and Enrico Fermi in Italy.

In 1934, Fermi thought he had created element 93. As part of a broader experiment, he and his team had systematically irradiated one element after another in an attempt to make them radioactive. Each element being tested was simply placed next to radioactive materials that gave off neutrons. Finally, when he got to uranium, Fermi hoped that the nucleus would absorb the neutron and change into a new heavier manmade element. When he finished the experiment, he concluded that he had come up with element 93, along with a bewildering array of other particles that he couldn't identify.

When they heard about Fermi's findings, other research teams began experiments of their own. Meitner and Hahn had last worked together 12 years earlier, but Meitner wanted to collaborate with Hahn on this project because she trusted him. These tests demanded the skills of both a physicist and a chemist, preferably an expert radiochemist who could identify new and extremely heavy elements when only a few atoms would be available for analysis.

After weeks of persuasion, Hahn finally agreed to participate. He brought along a young analytical chemist, Fritz Strassmann. The team of Meitner, Hahn, and Strassmann had a remarkably productive period from 1934 to 1936, publishing eight articles about extraheavy transuranic elements during that time. As a chemist, Hahn was delighted to study new elements. Meitner's nephew, physicist Otto Robert Frisch, said, "For Hahn it was like the old days when new elements fell like apples when you shook the tree."

In France, Irène Joliot-Curie was on the same quest. After winning the Nobel Prize for discovering artificial radioactivity, the research team (but not the marriage) of Irène and Frédéric broke up. Frédéric received a job offer from the Collège de France, the most prestigious research institution in the country, and he took it. The Collège de France had space for him to build a cyclotron, an early type of particle accelerator—a sophisticated machine that uses magnetic forces to manipulate the speed of subatomic particles—and he realized that nuclear physicists would need accelerators to split open the nucleus of an atom. Frédéric also wanted to show the world that he could succeed without Irène. Irène became a professor at the University of Paris and continued as research director at the Radium Institute. She began working with another partner, Paul Savitch, a young Yugoslavian physicist.

Irène and Meitner—as well as others—were performing experiments to create transuranic elements, and they were all getting different, puzzling results. Everyone expected the uranium to absorb the neutron and become an even heavier element. But Irène and Savitch bombarded uranium with neutrons and found an element that resembled the known element lanthanum (atomic number 57), which is much lighter than uranium. Meitner, Hahn, and Strassmann bombarded uranium with neutrons and found an element that resembled barium (atomic number 56). An Italian physicist on Fermi's team said: "The first thing Hahn and Meitner did was to confirm all

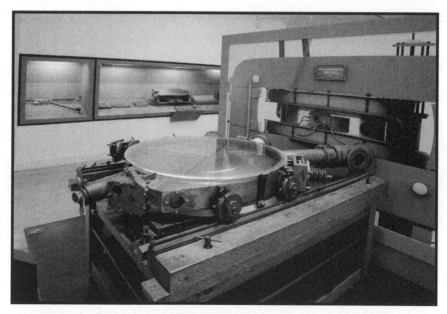

A French cyclotron similar to one Frédéric Joliot-Curie may have wanted. A cyclotron is a type of particle accelerator or "atom smasher" that uses electromagnetic fields to speed up subatomic particles in physics experiments. In many cases, scientists smash the particles together at great speed to study the collisions and learn more about the nature of matter and energy.

our results . . . and the more experiments they did, the more things became 'strange.' You see, they started to find things that looked like lanthanum and radium, and the whole thing became more and more complicated and messy."

"Curiousium"

Why were research teams getting such inconsistent and unexpected results? In many of the experiments, the researchers were creating isotopes, a variation of an element that has the same number of protons (so it has the same atomic number), but a different number of neutrons (which gives it a different atomic weight, the sum of the number of protons and neutrons). Radioactive elements decay from one isotope to another until they become stable. This step-by-step process of transformation is called a *decay series* or a *decay chain*.

The research on uranium yielded confusing findings. Researchers tried to classify the new substances based on their chemical behavior, but it wasn't easy. No one knew exactly what to expect or predict. The researchers assumed they would find new elements that would simply extend the periodic table, but the transuranic products defied classification.

The competition between research teams became more heated. Although they were colleagues, Meitner and Irène were not friends. They had met at scientific conferences, but they formed no special kinship as the leading women scientists in their field. In early May 1935, Hahn and Meitner announced the discovery of a radioactive decay series for thorium. Later the same month, Irène and her team announced that they, too, had discovered the missing series, but they had different results.

First, Meitner and Hahn were annoyed that Irène had not adequately credited them in a recently published paper. Hahn wanted professional credit because he felt vulnerable at that time in Nazi Germany, where his future seemed unpredictable. Referring to the political situation and the importance of protecting his reputation, Hahn wrote: "We regret this very much, for a scientific echo has never been as necessary to us as just now." In addition, Hahn was aware that without professional recognition, Meitner, a person of Jewish heritage, was at greater risk in the increasingly hostile environment in Germany.

The issue of academic credit aside, Meitner and Irène were challenging each other head-on, each side insisting that the other was wrong. Theories about the structure and nature of the nucleus were based on experimental evidence, not observable information. Meitner was known for examining data and developing theories to explain the results. Irène's results didn't fit Meitner's possible theories, so Meitner had assumed that there was something wrong with Irène's experimental design. In this case, Meitner asked a former graduate student to double-check Irène's work by searching for alpha particles that should have been emitted if Irène had been correct. He did not find any.

Meitner also dismissed Irène's results as faulty because she and Savitch reported finding a short-lived byproduct that resembled an isotope of thorium. Irène's team measured the activity of the substance without first chemically separating it the way that Meitner's team did. Using their approach, Irène's team found the same decay pattern that Meitner had found, plus the additional thorium isotope, which the Germans apparently had overlooked.

In all of the experiments they had done on transuranics, Meitner and Hahn had never found this byproduct. Meitner would not accept that she had spent years working on this question and had never encountered this mystery isotope. Meitner asked Strassmann to search for thorium, and he didn't find it. Convinced that Irène was wrong, Meitner didn't continue to look for the thorium isotope.

Meitner felt confident that her team's chemistry was better than that of the French team. Meitner said that Irène was "still relying on the chemical knowledge she received from her famous mother and that knowledge is just a bit out of date today." Instead of taking Irène's work seriously, Hahn mockingly named Curie's new substance "curiousium."

Meitner didn't want to embarrass Irène in print, so on January 20, 1938, Meitner and Hahn wrote to Irène, presenting the details of their own experiments and suggesting that she had "committed a gross error." They said that they would not embarrass her with public criticism if she would simply make a "public retraction" of her findings.

In the next round of publications, Irène acknowledged Meitner's letter and retracted that she had found a thorium isotope, but she reported that she had repeated the experiment and again found the same substance, only this time she thought it might be actinium.

Frustrated by the ongoing debate, Meitner gave up. Strassmann wrote: "[Meitner] lost interest in the situation. She could rightfully point to the fact that it would be tremendously improbable for slow neutrons to knock out alpha particles *and* protons from uranium." In addition, Meitner and her team had never observed any alpha particles in their work. Meitner kept working, ignoring Irène's research and assuming Irène was wrong.

A few months later, Hahn saw Frédéric at the Tenth International Congress of Chemistry in Rome. Hahn pulled Frédéric aside and said, "Between us, my dear, it's because your wife is a woman that I haven't permitted myself to criticize her. But she is wrong, and I intend to prove it."

When Irène heard about Hahn's comment, she repeated her experiment, and, when she got the same result, she published it again. This time the article not only reaffirmed the existence of the new substance, it also reported that the substance behaved like lanthanum, nearly halfway down the periodic table from uranium. They concluded that it "cannot be anything except a transuranic element, possessing very different [chemical] properties from the other known transuranics, a hypothesis which raises great difficulties for its interpretation."

Strassmann encouraged Meitner and Hahn to take Irène's work seriously. Hahn repeated his experiment, using Irène's methods, and this time they, too, found the unusual isotope.

What was going on?

Hahn wondered whether they were somehow creating radium, with atomic number 88. To test his theory, Hahn and Meitner devised an experiment using (nonradioactive) barium to help them separate out and measure radioactive radium. They knew that radium and barium always separated out of chemical compounds together.

But before she could carry out the experiment, Meitner had to flee Nazi Germany.

10

FLEEING HITLER'S GERMANY

A LL LISE MEITNER wanted was to be left alone to work on her transuranic research in peace. She had tried to ignore politics and focus on her scientific work, but in Hitler's Germany in the 1930s, there was no way for her to avoid it.

The trouble had begun on January 30, 1933, when Adolf Hitler was sworn in as Germany's new chancellor. After World War I, Germany had been governed by the Weimar Republic, a liberal government that increased personal rights and freedoms, but Germany was devastated by the global economic depression of 1929. Faced with economic insecurity and vulnerability, many Germans supported Hitler's National Socialist Party, also known as the Nazis. Nazis believed that so-called Aryans (Germans and those of European and Western Asian heritage) were part of a superior master race. They blamed other non-Aryan people, as they defined them—especially Jews—for Germany's problems.

By 1932, Hitler had been elected chancellor, and he initiated programs he said would reestablish national pride and reclaim Germany's rightful position in the world.

The Aryan Race

When Hitler took office, he began a campaign against all "non-Aryans," paying special attention to Jews and those of Jewish descent. Under Hitler's rule, anyone with one or more Jewish grandparents was considered Jewish. All four of Meitner's grandparents had been Jewish, so she was Jewish under Nazi law, even though she had converted to Christianity as a young woman shortly after moving to Berlin.

A few months after Hitler became chancellor, he issued the "Law for the Restoration of the Professional Civil Service," which banned non-Aryans from working for the state, including public universities. At first, Meitner wasn't concerned. She was an Austrian citizen, not a German, and she assumed her foreign status would protect her. In the years since the war, Germany had gone through a number of social and political movements, so she may have assumed that Hitler's policies would be a passing phase, too. She focused on her research at the Institute and her teaching at the University of Berlin, without giving much thought to Hitler or his political campaigns.

In the months that followed, Hitler and his Nazi leadership became bolder. Jewish intellectuals and scientists were forced to resign from their jobs. This new reality hit home for Meitner when Nazi officials demanded that Fritz Haber, a German Jew, step down as director of the Kaiser Wilhelm Institute for Physical Chemistry. In his April 30, 1933, letter of resignation, Haber wrote:

> According to the law of April 1, 1933, I am derived from Jewish parents and grandparents . . . I tender my resignation with the same pride with which I have served my country during my lifetime. . . . For more than forty years I have selected my collaborators on the basis of their intelligence and their character and not on the basis of their grandmothers, and I am not willing for the rest of my life to change this method, which I have found so good.

The new director, Gerhart Jander, had very little research experience, but he was a loyal Nazi, so he got the job.

In the laboratory, Meitner and her coworkers discussed Haber's resignation. Max Planck, director of the Institute, felt conflicted about how to handle the situation. He didn't agree with the law, but he was a loyal German who believed in his government. After the fact, Meitner said, "Planck once said, truly desperately, 'But what should I do? It is the law.' And when I said: 'But how can something so lawless be a law?' he seemed visibly relieved." Like Planck, during this early period of Hitler's administration, many Germans struggled to know how to respond to political decrees they didn't support.

Meitner urged Planck to intervene on Haber's behalf and try to help him get his job back. Planck, as president of the Kaiser Wilhelm Society, arranged to meet with Hitler to discuss the matter. Planck reflected on this awkward meeting years later in an article titled "My Meeting with Hitler." He wrote: "Hitler answered me literally: 'I have nothing against the Jews. But the Jews are all Communists, and these are my enemies. My life is against them.'"

Planck responded by saying that many "old families" of impeccable German heritage were, in fact, Jews. Hitler went into a rage, screaming: "That is not right. A Jew is a Jew. All Jews hang together. Where one Jew is, there are others of their species." Hitler ranted; Planck sat in stunned silence.

At the first opportunity to leave, Planck excused himself, more concerned than ever about the plight of Jewish people living in Germany. Planck no longer viewed Hitler as a rational leader, and Plank never again intervened for any member of the Kaiser Wilhelm Society. Instead, Planck kept to himself and tried to avoid notice until his death, several years after the end of the war.

Meitner may have considered leaving Germany, but she had built a life there. Her work and her friends were in Berlin, and—at least at that time—she thought she was safe. Planck encouraged Meitner to stay at the Institute as long as possible, explaining that her job was secure because German Civil Service Laws did not apply to her since she was an Austrian citizen. Many Jewish and part-Jewish scientists left Germany at that time, but others stayed and hoped that the political situation would soon return to normal.

Instead of improving, however, things got worse. Meitner spent the summer of 1933 in Vienna, visiting with family. While she was there she received a questionnaire from the German Ministry of Education that asked about the race of her four grandparents. Meitner did not consider herself Jewish; she thought of herself as a Protestant with Jewish ancestors. After all, she had never practiced Judaism. Meitner completed the form honestly, acknowledging that all four of her grandparents were Jewish. She still assumed that her Austrian citizenship would protect her job.

On September 6, 1933, bad news arrived. Meitner received notice from the Prussian Minister of Education that referred directly

Adolf Hitler at the window of the Chancellery in Berlin while the crowds below applaud him on the evening of his swearing in as chancellor.

to the questionnaire she had filled out. It said: "Immediately! For the reason set forth in paragraph 3 of the statute concerning the reinstatement of the professional civil service, I hereby revoke your authorization of professorship at the University of Berlin."

Meitner was shocked and confused. It didn't make sense to her: What difference did it make that her grandmothers were Jewish? She had lectured at the university for more than 15 years. She was an Austrian citizen. She had complied with the laws and avoided any confrontation with the Nazis.

At that point, Meitner still had her work at the Institute, but she could no longer participate in any university activities, including the Wednesday colloquia. She could not publish articles or attend conferences or teach her classes. When Hahn presented a talk outside the Institute about his work with Meitner, he could not mention her by name. If she remained in Germany, her professional reputation would be erased. But even if Meitner had considered leaving Germany, she had no idea where to go.

"Jewish Physics"

As time went on, the German government became progressively more repressive. On September 15, 1935, the Nuremberg Laws were passed, depriving all Jewish people of their German citizenship.

The government declared "German physics" superior to "Jewish physics," and banned the discussion of all ideas developed by Jews or scientists of Jewish descent. This ban on Jewish physics made the Wednesday colloquia so dull that one of Meitner's assistants, the future Nobel Prize–winning molecular biologist Max Delbrück, organized private meetings at his mother's house so that all scientists could talk openly about physics and biology, without worrying about politics or who might be listening.

Meitner stayed in Germany after her university post was revoked because she thought she was "too valuable to annoy." When it became clear that she, too, was vulnerable to discrimination by the Nazis, Meitner stayed because she felt supported by her community. She and her coworkers at the Institute felt "a very strong feeling of solidarity between us, built on mutual trust, which made it possible for the work to continue quite undisturbed even after 1933, although the staff was not entirely united in its political views. . . . It was something quite exceptional in the political conditions of that day." In 1935, Niels Bohr, a physicist friend in Sweden, arranged a Rockefeller Foundation grant for Meitner to leave Germany and spend a year in Copenhagen, but Planck urged Meitner to turn it down and stay in Germany because he valued her contributions to his lab. She did.

The longer Meitner stayed in Germany, the harder it became for her to find a job in another country. For one thing, so many other scientists had left to take jobs overseas that fewer positions were available. In addition, Nazi officials were turning up the pressure to have Meitner fired from the Institute. Hahn was caught in the middle, and he worried that he might lose his job as director of his section of the lab.

Meitner thought Hahn should take a stand against Nazism, but he was cautious and quiet about the issue. He didn't want to risk his professional standing, and he didn't believe his lone voice would make any difference. "As long as it's only us [the Jews] who have the sleepless night and not you, it will not be any better in Germany," Meitner often told him.

Meitner sympathized with Hahn somewhat because she, too, had avoided facing the realities of the political situation for as long as possible. "The years of the Hitler regime . . . were naturally very depressing," Meitner wrote years later. "But work was a good friend, and I have often thought and said how wonderful it is that by work one may be granted a long respite of forgetfulness from oppressive political conditions." When Meitner later became aware of the atrocities that had occurred under the Nazis, including the death of six million Jewish people, she said, "It was not only stupid but also very wrong that I did not leave at once."

From Austrian Christian to German Jew

On March 12, 1938, Germany invaded Austria. Overnight, Meitner lost her legal status as an Austrian citizen, since her homeland no longer existed as a sovereign country. She went to bed as an Austrian Christian and woke up a German Jew, stripped of all her rights of citizenship.

Meitner was trapped; she had stayed too long in Hitler's Germany. On a day-to-day basis, she maintained her routines at the Institute and tried to keep a low profile. She avoided the staff members who had joined the Nazi Party and supported Hitler. Kurt Hess, a vocal Nazi member who headed a small guest department on the top floor of the Institute, harassed people who supported Meitner or sympathized with her situation. He often said: "The Jewess endangers this Institute . . . she must go."

Hahn and other administrators within the Kaiser Wilhelm Society debated about what to do with Meitner. Eventually, her case came up before the Reich Research Council and Hahn was forced to decide whether or not to argue for her to stay. "I rather lost my nerve," Hahn said years after the event. Instead of defending Meitner, he discussed her resignation from the Institute.

> In a conversation with [the Institute treasurer] I spoke of Lise Meitner and the new awkward situation since the annexation of Austria. [He] suggested that Lise might resign from her position because nothing more could be done; perhaps she could continue working unofficially. I do not exactly remember the concrete proposals. Unfortunately, I told Lise about that conversation. Lise was very unhappy and angry with me, because now I had let her down.

Meitner's diary from that time was more direct. She wrote that the treasurer of the Institute demanded that she leave. "Hahn says I must not come to the Institute anymore." The following day, she went to the Institute to record the results of a neutron irradiation experiment, and Hahn asked her to go home. "He has in essence thrown me out," she wrote.

Hahn defended his stand. "I always remembered that Lise would have to give up her position [eventually] because she must see that she endangered the Institute," Hahn said. Meitner didn't see herself as a threat; she was hurt and offended that Hahn had put the Institute and his job there ahead of her

German and Austrian border police tearing down a gate after Nazi Germany annexed Austria in March 1938.

personal welfare. Several days later the treasurer reversed his decision and allowed Meitner to return to her lab, but Meitner did not forget that Hahn had refused to back her up when she needed him most.

Although Hahn didn't come to Meitner's defense, the president of the Kaiser Wilhelm Society, who greatly admired Meitner, asked the Minister of Education to let her go to a neutral country, such as Sweden, Denmark, or Switzerland. The response shocked them all. The Minister responded:

It is considered undesirable that renowned Jews should leave Germany for abroad to act there against the interests of

Germany according to their inner persuasion as representatives of the German sciences. . . . The Kaiser Wilhelm Society will certainly find a way for Professor Meitner to stay in Germany after her retirement. . . .

Not long after Meitner received the letter, she heard from her friend, Max von Laue, that the office of the Chief of the Secret Police was about to announce a new law that would prohibit all university graduates—Jewish or not—from leaving Germany. If she stayed in Berlin, it was a matter of time before Meitner would be arrested. If she was going to leave Germany, she had to get out right away.

The Escape

To avoid arrest, Meitner left her apartment and moved into the Hotel Adlon where she thought she would be safer, at least for the moment. As the situation became dire, friends and colleagues outside of Germany began to offer to help get Meitner out of the country. Colleagues in Switzerland, Holland, and Denmark invited her to give seminars and attend conferences or do anything else that might provide an official excuse to leave Germany.

Niels Bohr wrote a carefully crafted letter to Meitner:

The local Physical Society and the Chemistry Association have delegated me to ask you if you would give their members the great pleasure and generous instruction by holding a seminar in the near future concerning your very fruitful investigations of the artificially induced new radioactive family of radioactive elements. As to the date, we can entirely accommodate ourselves to your convenience. . . .

The letter gave Meitner complete flexibility to arrange a time and date for travel that met her needs.

Niels Bohr, 1935. Bohr was among many colleagues who supported Lise Meitner as she made arrangements to flee Nazi Germany.

In early May, Meitner accepted Bohr's invitation to work at his institute in Copenhagen. The Bohrs were close friends of hers, and her favorite nephew, Otto Robert Frisch, was working there as well. Her plans stalled when she tried to get a travel visa and found that her Austrian passport was no longer valid, so she could not get the necessary travel documents.

Meitner didn't realize it at the time, but Bohr had asked for help from two other physicists in Holland, Adriaan Fokker and Dirk Coster. They immediately began raising money necessary for Meitner to be hired to teach in the Netherlands. A worldwide depression made it difficult to gather the funds, but plans were underway for Meitner's escape to Holland.

While the Dutch team was making arrangements, another escape plan was being devised. Swedish physicist Manne Siegbahn, who was building a new Research Institute for Physics near the University of Stockholm, had worked with Meitner in the early 1920s. He agreed to offer Meitner a position at his new Institute. He wanted to let Meitner know about his offer, but government censors monitored all letters entering the country. In order to communicate the plan to Meitner, in June Siegbahn sent a messenger to Berlin to speak with her directly.

Day by day, the situation in Germany grew more dangerous. In Holland, Dirk Coster decided that Meitner needed to get out of Germany right away, even if she did not have a job lined up. Coster was in poor health and he was the father of four children, but he had put himself at risk by helping a number of Jewish-German refugees since 1933. On June 27, 1938, Coster wrote to Fokker and reported that he considered the situation urgent enough that he would no longer wait for the Dutch government to approve the necessary paperwork; he was going to go to Germany and he planned to travel back to the Netherlands with Meitner.

Coster wired Peter Debye, the new head of the Kaiser Wilhelm Institute for Physics, and spoke in a pre-arranged code: He said that he was coming to Berlin to interview an "assistant"—meaning Meitner—to whom he could "offer a one-year appointment."

Unfortunately, the Dutch team didn't know that the Swedes were planning a similar rescue effort. On the same day that Coster arrived in Berlin, Siegbahn sent a member of the Swedish Academy of Sciences to Berlin to offer Meitner a one-year salaried position in Stockholm. Debye told Meitner about the Dutch offer just after she heard about the Swedish one. Meitner wasn't sure what to do, but she decided to accept the offer to go to Stockholm because she had spoken to them first. In addition, nuclear physics was just getting started in Sweden, so she felt she had an opportunity to do more useful work there. At the time, Meitner had no idea of the trouble her friends in Holland had gone through to help her. She also didn't realize that she was in immediate danger.

On June 30, her situation changed again. She learned that her position in Sweden had not been finalized, and that her visa was not in order. She could not leave for Sweden after all.

Meitner didn't know what to do, so she continued her work at the Institute. She spent long hours in the lab with Hahn and Strassmann discussing their transuranic results. In the meantime, Debye contacted Coster again to see if he still wanted an "assistant." He wrote about Meitner as if she were a male assistant: "The assistant we talked about, who had made what seemed like a firm decision, sought me out once again. . . . He is now completely convinced (this happened in the last few days) that he would rather go to Groningen, indeed that this is the only avenue open to him. . . ."

In the Netherlands, Coster immediately recognized the urgency of the situation. He sent a telegraph: "SAT 9 JULY / I AM COMING TO LOOK OVER THE ASSISTANT: IF HE SUITS ME I WILL TAKE HIM BACK WITH ME." He then telegraphed Fokker, who contacted The Hague, where the Dutch Ministry of Justice had received the appeal for Meitner's entry papers twelve days before.

It was Saturday, so the Ministry was closed. Fokker turned to the office of the Dutch Border Guards and met with the director, who promised him an answer on Monday. Coster spent all day Sunday waiting for a reply from the authorities. In an attempt to make sure that Meitner would be able to cross the border successfully even though she had only an Austrian passport, Coster traveled to the border town of Nieuweschans and met personally with immigration officers there. (He had arranged for Meitner to travel on a route that crossed the border at the small station where the security would be less intense.) Coster showed them Meitner's official entrance permit from The Hague and he asked them to use "friendly persuasion" with the German border guards to let her through.

On Monday morning, July 11, Fokker's phone rang. The Ministry had granted Meitner provisional admission, and written confirmation was being forwarded. Coster left for Berlin that night by train. On board, Nazi soldiers were everywhere, and passports were checked and rechecked when the travelers reached the border. Coster noted how different that landscape looked: Flags with swastikas waved from the medieval buildings in every little town the train went through.

Back in Berlin, Meitner still did not know the plan. She thought she was waiting for confirmation that she was approved for travel to Stockholm. On July 12, 1938, a hot and humid Tuesday, she arrived early at the Institute of Chemistry. Hahn called her into his office, told her that arrangements had been made for her to leave for Holland the next day.

Stunned, Meitner agreed to work a normal day, and then go back to her room and pack as if she were going on a summer vacation. She would not have a chance to say good-bye, even to friends and colleagues she had known for more than 30 years. She could not take her notebooks or scientific papers or any laboratory equipment. It had to appear that she was just going on a short vacation. She had only 10 marks in her purse.

On her last night in Germany, Meitner worked at the Institute until eight o'clock, proofreading a paper to be published by one of her students. Afterward, she went to her room and packed two small suitcases, and then she went to Hahn's house to stay with his family. She did not check out of the hotel, but Hahn knew that she would not be safe in her room if the authorities learned of her planned departure.

The next morning, Wednesday, July 13, Meitner had to say good-bye to Hahn, her longtime friend and partner. At the moment of their farewell, Hahn gave Meitner a diamond ring that had belonged to his mother. She was to use it "for urgent emergencies." In other words, she was to use it to bribe the border guards if it came to that.

Meitner got in the car to drive to the train station. On the way, she lost her nerve: She panicked and begged the driver, Paul Rosbaud, a physicist friend, to turn back. Instead, he comforted her and reassured her that this way the only way she would be safe—and he kept going. Once she had composed herself, Rosbaud took Meitner into the terminal, which was crowded with Nazi and Secret Service officers. Meitner boarded the train alone; Coster, her traveling companion, discreetly boarded the train after Meitner and accompanied her from a distance. They were safer traveling separately, in case one or the other was taken into custody.

On the seven-hour trip to the Dutch border, Meitner experienced absolute terror. Although Coster had arranged with the border guards ahead of time to let her enter the country, there was a chance that she would not be allowed to cross the border. She knew the danger: Time after time people who tried to escape from Germany had been arrested and brought back.

At each stop along the way, German police checked identity papers. Several passengers were arrested and removed from the train. A Nazi military patrol studied her travel documents for ten minutes as Meitner sat frozen in fear. She did not have a valid passport or entry visa. Eventually, the Dutch guards looked down at her over the shoulders of the German officers and then passed her by.

She crossed the border without incident.

Once in the Netherlands, she could relax somewhat. The train traveled for several hours more before arriving in Groningen, where she would be staying. Exhausted and relieved beyond measure, Meitner and Coster met each other in the small train station. Coster picked up her bags and took her to his car.

Meitner had been in more danger than she had realized. Kurt Hess, the Nazi loyalist at the Institute, had found out about her escape plans and notified the authorities. If she had delayed her travel by even a few hours, she would likely have been arrested.

Nine years later, Meitner was interviewed and asked about the escape. She said:

I took a train for Holland on the pretext that I wanted to spend a week's vacation. At the Dutch border, I got the scare of my life when a Nazi military patrol of five men going through the coaches picked up my Austrian passport, which had expired long ago. I got so frightened, my heart almost stopped beating. I knew that the Nazis had just declared open season on Jews, that the hunt was on. For ten minutes I sat there and waited, ten minutes that seemed like so many hours. Then one of the Nazi officials returned and handed me back the passport without a word. Two minutes later I descended on Dutch territory, where I was met by some of my Holland colleagues.

The day after her arrival in Holland, Coster sent Hahn a telegram using a prearranged code. He said that the "baby" had arrived safely.

Hahn wired back: "I want to congratulate you. What will be the name of your darling daughter?"

Now that the mission had been completed, Coster received a flood of congratulations from the international scientific community. Physicist Wolfgang Pauli wired from Switzerland: "YOU HAVE MADE YOURSELF AS FAMOUS FOR THE ABDUCTION OF LISE MEITNER AS FOR [the discovery of] HAFNIUM!"

Once she settled in, Coster sent news of Meitner's safe arrival to their network of friends. She didn't expect to have been put in this situation, but she was grateful for all that others had done to help her escape. In that moment, she wasn't sure what the future held for her: She was almost 60 years old and starting her life over again. She had no idea that the most important scientific discovery of her life was still ahead.

EUREKA!
THE DISCOVERY
OF FISSION

LTHOUGH SHE WAS safe from the threats she faced in Nazi Germany, Meitner found it difficult to settle into her new life. She first sought refuge in Groningen in the Netherlands, but after several weeks she moved on to Sweden to work at Manne Sieg-bahn's institute in Stockholm. In hindsight, Meitner's decision to leave the Netherlands was a wise one; within two years, it would be taken over by the Nazis just as Austria had been.

Meitner still felt homesick and heartsick. She missed the fellowship of her friends and colleagues and the familiarity of her apartment and her belongings. During the Arctic winter, Meitner found the days too short and the nights too long, and she felt like a stranger when she walked the streets, still unaccustomed to the language and traditions of her new country. The weather had turned cold and she had only her summer clothes. Her bank account had been frozen in Berlin, so she was financially dependent on other people. Most of all, she missed the work she loved: In Germany, she had been the director of her own department; in Stockholm, she worked as a researcher in someone else's laboratory.

When Meitner arrived in Sweden, she contacted Hahn to officially sever ties with the Institute and ask for the pension she had earned based on 30 years of work. On August 24, 1938, she wrote to Hahn:

> I am sure no day will pass when I shall not think with gratitude and longing of our friendship, our joint work, and the Institute. But I don't belong there any longer, and when I reflect on the last months, it seems to me that my retirement will also comply with the wishes of the staff. It's no use talking about it too much: The facts are facts, you cannot pass them over. . . . In my inner self I have not yet quite realized that what I have just written is real, but it is real.

"The Best and Most Beautiful Part of My Life"

At the Institute, two former colleagues—both Nazi Party members—wanted to take over Meitner's position now that she was gone. In a letter to Meitner, Hahn told her that one of them wondered if she had lost her nerve by leaving Germany. Meitner was furious. She wrote to Hahn:

> If [the former colleague] asks whether I have lost my nerve, it is because he thinks I have abandoned my responsibilities. . . . They must surely think I evaded my responsibilities if you do not explicitly tell them it was impossible for me to stay. . . . My future is cut off, shall the past also be taken from me? . . . I have done nothing wrong, why should I suddenly be treated like a nonperson, or worse, someone who is buried alive?

Hahn was shocked at Meitner's response and her apparent ignorance of the recent events in Germany. Hahn's wife had suffered a nervous breakdown and was held in a sanatorium, and his

16-year-old son had been compelled to join the Hitler Youth. He wrote back: "Can you seriously think that anyone considers you a deserter? . . . Believe me, I know it is hard to be of good cheer when everything is so new. But you are perhaps too optimistic about our current good fortune here."

Meitner still worried that her former coworkers had lost confidence in her. She wrote to Hahn:

> I had regarded this work together as the best and most beautiful part of my life, and it hurts me to think these people might now think I left them in the lurch. . . . Don't be bitter or angry, we want to help each other, not make things worse for each other than they already are.

In Sweden, Meitner began working at Siegbahn's Nobel-funded Physics Institute, but she didn't feel welcome there. She was just learning Swedish, and many of her colleagues made little effort to speak slowly or to include her in conversation. She wanted to continue her work on transuranic elements, but she didn't have the equipment or support she needed for her work. She earned very little, about the same pay as a junior assistant just starting out. Frustrated and alone, Meitner wrote to Hahn again on September 25, 1938:

> Perhaps you cannot fully appreciate how unhappy it makes me to realize that you always think that I am unfair and embittered, and that you also say so to other people. If you think it over, it cannot be difficult to understand what it means that I have none of my scientific equipment. For me that is much harder than everything else. But I am really not embittered—it is just that I see no real purpose in my life at the moment and I am very lonely. . . . Work can hardly be thought of. There is [no equipment] for doing experiments, and in the entire building just four young physicists and very bureaucratic working rules.

As the months passed, things didn't get much better. During the fall, when Meitner learned Hahn was going to be in Sweden visiting Niels Bohr, she made the eight-hour train trip to Copenhagen to meet with him to discuss their work on transuranic elements. Hahn couldn't stay long—back in Germany his wife was on the verge of another mental breakdown—but he wanted to consult with Meitner about the work he and Strassmann were doing. After a tearful reunion, Meitner analyzed his findings and encouraged him to go back and repeat certain experiments.

Hahn was fortunate to have been out of the country at that time. The evening before—on November 9, 1938—Hitler's Nazi Party shattered the lives of thousands of people on a spree of violence and evil that was to become known as Kristallnacht, the Night of Broken Glass. During the overnight hours, Hitler's Security Service destroyed the homes and businesses of Jews, and thousands were rounded up, arrested, and taken to concentration camps.

Three days later, the Nazis stripped all Jews in Germany of their rights to business or cultural life. Beginning on November 15, Jewish children were forbidden from attending school. Jews were required to wear a yellow star badge on their sleeve. All Jews were renamed, with either "Sarah" or "Israel" added to their names for their identification as Jews. Meitner's lawyer changed all of her legal documents from Lise Meitner to Lise Sarah Meitner in accordance with the law.

Meitner worried about her family left behind in German-controlled Vienna. Her brother-in-law, Justinian (Jutz) Frisch, a well-known lawyer in Vienna, had been arrested and sent to a concentration camp in Dachau, Germany. Meitner made plans for his wife, her sister Auguste, to join her in Stockholm where she would be safer. (Several months later, Jutz was released from Dachau and joined Meitner and Auguste in Sweden.)

At the end of the year, Meitner was even more discouraged. On December 5, 1938, in a letter to Hahn, she complained: "I often

A demolished storefront in November 1938 following Kristallnacht, the Night of Broken Glass.

feel like a wound-up puppet that does certain things, gives a friendly smile, and has no real life in itself."

The Secret Partner

Despite the growing tension in Germany, Hahn and Meitner continued to correspond and collaborate on their research. Even though she wasn't present in the lab and Hahn did not say her name aloud, Meitner continued to influence Hahn's work: She had designed the experiments on transuranic elements that Hahn and Strassmann were carrying out, and they were using the equipment she had built and had been forced to leave behind.

Strassmann, a shy and gifted chemist, did not support Hitler and refused to join any Nazi organizations. Hahn hired him because of his talent in the laboratory, but Strassmann was virtually unemployable in private industry because of his politics. In fact, during the war, he, his wife, and their small child secretly sheltered a Jew in their apartment, even though this act of defiance would have cost his family dearly if they had been discovered. Strassmann sympathized with Meitner's plight and respected her as a colleague.

Hahn did not tell anyone at the Institute—including Strassmann—about his meeting with Meitner. Still, Strassmann considered Meitner the intellectual leader of their team, even though she lived in a different country. "On all very difficult questions and calculations in physics, Hahn consulted Meitner," said Günter Herrmann, a friend of Strassmann. "The guidance of Lise Meitner over the four years is obvious."

Christmas Holiday

Christmas was approaching, but Meitner remained fearful and depressed about her situation. To raise Meitner's spirits, Eva von Bahr-Bergius invited her dear friend to join her in Kungälv, a quaint village on the Swedish coast. She also invited Meitner's nephew, Otto Robert Frisch, to come up from Copenhagen.

Just before Meitner left for the holiday, she received a letter from Hahn. Meitner and Hahn exchanged letters almost every other day and the Berlin-Stockholm mail was typically delivered overnight. On the night of December 19, 1938, Hahn wrote to Meitner about the series of experiments involving transuranic elements he and Strassmann had completed three days before:

> It is now practically eleven o'clock at night. Strassmann will be coming back at 11:45 so that I can get home at long last. The thing is: there is something so odd about the "radium isotopes" that for the moment we don't want to tell anyone but you. The half-lives of the three isotopes are pretty accurately determined; they can be separated from all the elements except barium: all processes are correct. Except for

one—unless there are some very weird accidental circumstances involved, fractionalization doesn't work. Our radium
isotopes behave like barium. . . .

The letter continued:

> Perhaps you can suggest some fantastic explanation. We
> understand that it really *can't* break up into barium. . . . So
> try to think of some other possibility. Barium isotopes with
> much higher atomic weights than 137? If you can think of
> anything that might be publishable, then the three of us
> would be together in this work after all. We don't believe this
> is foolishness or that contaminations are playing tricks on us.

Meitner received Hahn's Monday-night letter in Stockholm on
Wednesday, December 21. She found the news almost unbelievable.
If they were correct, then that meant that the uranium nucleus must
be fracturing. She wrote him back:

> Your radium results are very amazing. A process that works
> with slow neutrons and leads to barium! . . . To me for the
> time being the hypothesis of such an extensive burst seems
> very difficult to accept, but we have experienced so many
> surprises in nuclear physics that one cannot say without
> hesitation of anything: "It's impossible."

Meitner couldn't get Hahn's letter out of her mind, but she continued with her plans to travel to Kungälv on Friday. She told Hahn
to address his next letter to her there, but he did not receive this
message in time.

Hahn and Strassmann finished their experiment and confirmed
that they had identified lanthanum from barium decay. He wrote
to Meitner again, asking her to try to come up with a theory that
might explain the unexpected and unprecedented results of his experiments. Instead of waiting for her response, however, Hahn felt

pressure to publish his results. He sent his article to the German journal, *Die Naturwissenschaften*, on December 22, 1938. At the same time, Hahn mailed Meitner a carbon copy of the article. Meitner wasn't given any credit in the published work, but it was politically impossible for Meitner to be a joint author on the article, since it would have been a public admission that she and Hahn had been working together illegally. The article was to be published on January 6, 1939.

Hahn hurried to press because he worried that someone else—perhaps the Joliot-Curies—may very well have made the same discovery, and he did not want to give them a chance to publish their findings first. He wanted to release news of his test results, even if he could not offer a coherent theory to justify them. In other words, he could explain *what* happened in his experiment, but he couldn't explain *why* it happened.

Hahn wrote to Meitner:

> We cannot hush up the results, even though they may be absurd in physical terms. You can see that you will be performing a good deed if you find an alternative [explanation]. When we finish tomorrow or the day after I will send you a copy of the manuscript. . . . The whole thing is not very well suited for *Naturwissenschaften*. But they will publish it quickly.

Hahn mailed the letter to Meitner, but he sent it to the wrong address, so she did not receive it until after she returned from the holidays.

Hahn's article stopped short of reaching a clear conclusion. In it, he and Strassmann speculated that the uranium might be forming barium and other lighter elements, but it did not present a hypothesis explaining why this was happening. The key paragraph in the article stated:

From these experiments, we must, as chemists, rename the elements in the above scheme, and instead of radium, actinium, and thorium, write barium, lanthanum, and cerium. As "nuclear chemists" who are somewhat related to physicists, we cannot yet decide to take this big step, which contradicts all previous experiences of nuclear physics. It is still possible that we could have been misled by an unusual series of accidents.

Hahn was suggesting that the heavy uranium atoms were being divided into lighter elements. Rarely has such an important result been announced so indirectly and half-heartedly. Many readers wondered if Hahn and Strassmann even understood what they had found.

A Walk in the Woods

Two days before Christmas, Meitner arrived in Kungälv for the holidays, and she was joined by her nephew, Otto Robert Frisch. The following morning—Christmas Eve—Frisch came downstairs and showed his aunt his plans for a large magnet he intended to build for a research project involving the magnetic behavior of neutrons. Meitner looked them over, then steered the conversation around to Hahn's letter about transuranic elements.

She handed him Hahn's December 19 letter and insisted Frisch read it. He did. "Perhaps it is all wrong," Frisch said.

Meitner shook her head. "Hahn is too good a chemist," she answered. "I am sure this result is correct. But what on earth does it mean? How can one get a nucleus of barium from one of uranium?"

Frisch wanted to go cross-country skiing. Because Meitner had not brought her skis, she offered to walk beside him while he skied.

As she walked, Meitner explained that Hahn had found the particles produced by the uranium to be indistinguishable from barium.

She was an expert in nuclear theory and structure, and the results produced so far by transuranic research baffled her.

Meitner considered the facts: Uranium has 92 protons and barium has 56. How could uranium lose 36 protons all at once? Maybe a neutron could bump off one or two protons, but not 36.

Meitner kept walking. Could the uranium nucleus somehow be divided in two? She and Frisch knew that it was impossible for the uranium nuclei to have been broken in half. The year before, Niels Bohr had come up with a model of the nucleus that described it not as a brittle solid, but more like a drop of liquid.

That was it—the epiphany—the flash of insight that Meitner had been waiting for!

Frisch remembered the moment Meitner put the puzzle together. He said Meitner speculated:

> Perhaps a drop could divide itself into two SMALLER drops in a more gradual manner; first becoming elongated, then constricted, and finally, being torn rather than broken in two. We knew that there were strong forces which would resist such a process, just as the surface tension of an ordinary liquid drop resists its division into two smaller ones.

At first they thought that surface tension would hold the nucleus "drop" together, and then they considered that having 92 positively charged protons repelling each other would make a uranium nucleus electrically unstable so its surface tension would be weak. This theory also explained why no stable elements beyond uranium on the periodic table existed in nature. At higher levels the nucleus is so unstable it can't hold together.

Meitner and Frisch stopped walking and skiing. Frisch unstrapped his skis as Meitner brushed the snow off a log, and they sat down. Meitner pulled out a scrap of paper and pencil from her coat pocket and began to make calculations. Frisch recalled:

The charge of a uranium nucleus, we found, was indeed large enough to overcome the effect of the surface tension almost completely; so the uranium nucleus might indeed be a very wobbly, unstable drop, ready to divide itself at the slightest provocation, such as the impact of a neutron.

Meitner calculated that when one nucleus divided into two, the pair would be lighter than the original by approximately one-fifth the mass of a proton. She then applied Einstein's famous formula—$E=mc^2$—energy equals mass times the speed of light squared, and she found that one-fifth of a proton mass was equal to 200,000,000 electron volts of energy. On a larger scale, a single pound of uranium contained the energy equal to that produced by 40,000,000 pounds of TNT. Frisch recalled their triumph: "Here was the source for all that energy; it all fit!" For the first time, more energy came out of an experiment than went into it.

The numbers worked; the puzzle pieces fit together. The uranium nucleus behaved like a large water droplet. When overloaded by the extra neutron, the droplet—the nucleus—split in two. The drop could split into several different pairs: barium (56 protons) with krypton (36 protons), rubidium (37 protons) with cesium (55 protons), or any other pair of mid-sized atoms whose protons would total 92. That also explained why the Meitner team and the Joliot-Curie team had discovered so many different nuclei in their research.

Both Meitner and the Joliot-Curies had been right all along— but they had also both been wrong. Neither team had discovered the transuranic elements they were looking for, but they had both found pairs of elements that, when combined, were the same size as uranium.

How could some of the world's leading physicists have overlooked something so basic? First and most importantly, Meitner, the

Joliot-Curies, and other physicists exploring transuranic elements didn't discover fission earlier simply because they weren't looking for it. They were looking for heavy, transuranic elements, and that's what they thought that they had found. At the time, researchers assumed that when uranium was bombarded with neutrons it changed only slightly, by gaining or losing one or two protons at a time. No one considered the possibility that one oversized atom was dividing into two middle-sized atoms.

In science, it is essential both to isolate the evidence and to explain it. Hahn found the evidence, but Meitner is the one who made sense of it. Meitner knew that it would not take long for other researchers to understand and accept the idea of nuclear fission. The theory explained so much of what had seemed inexplicable about transuranic research for years. As is true with so many breakthrough ideas, the original insight was difficult to come up with, but once it was stated it seemed almost obvious.

CHAIN REACTION: RESEARCH ON FISSION GOES GLOBAL

A S 1938 DREW to a close, Lise Meitner cautiously accepted that fission was the only plausible explanation for the results of Otto Hahn's experiments. On January 1, 1939, she welcomed the New Year by writing a letter to Hahn: "[Frisch and I] have read your work very thoroughly and consider it perhaps possible energetically after all that such a heavy nucleus bursts." In other words, she had to come to terms with the reality that the uranium atoms had split in half after all.

Meitner had reservations about accepting the validity of fission because it meant that she and Hahn would have to retract their previous findings and announce that their work on transuranic elements had been wrong. Rather than boasting about making a history-changing discovery, Meitner was very worried that dismissing her previous work would compromise her reputation at her new job. After all, it would be an admission that nearly four years of work had been for nothing. Her New Year's letter continued: "You are in a much better position than I, since you and Strassmann have discovered it yourselves, while I only have years of work to refute—not a very good recommendation for my new beginning."

From the moment of Meitner's epiphany, not only did she understand how fission worked on a small scale, she also realized the possibility of using the energy from an initial division to create a chain reaction, in which the fission of one atom would trigger the fission of the next, on and on, releasing more and more energy with each nuclear division. If a controlled chain reaction could be created, then the process could be used to develop an explosion of unprecedented power. Meitner knew that her findings were of significant importance, especially in a world on the brink of war.

After returning from their vacation, Meitner and Frisch spoke on the telephone and began to work on a short article for the British journal *Nature*. They wanted to quickly share their findings with the world's scientific community, but they did not realize that Hahn had already notified a German scientific journal, and that his article would be published first.

Meitner also wrote to Hahn:

> Believe me, although I stand here with very empty hands, I am nevertheless happy for the wonder of these findings. . . . People will say that the three did nonsense and, now that one is gone, the other two made it right. . . . I am gradually losing all my courage. . . . Forgive this unhappy letter. I never wrote before how bad it really is. Sometimes I do not know what to do with my life. Most probably there are many people who have emigrated who feel as I do, but it is still very hard.

Meitner's words proved to be eerily accurate. Within a month Hahn began claiming that physics had impeded the discovery of fission and that chemistry alone had solved it—or, in other words, Meitner had interfered with a discovery that he had made on his own. At the time, Hahn felt insecure about his position at the Institute and believed that he needed the notoriety of a big discovery to secure his future employment. His status with the Nazis was tentative at best, and he constantly felt the need to defend himself and prove his worth. As he later said: "For me the uranium work [the discovery of fission] was a gift from heaven. Namely, I was fearful sometimes that [I would lose] part of the Institute."

Word Spreads

Frisch returned to Copenhagen after the holidays, and on January 3, he told his friend Niels Bohr about what he and Meitner had concluded about fission. "I had hardly begun to tell him," Frisch said, "when he struck his forehead with his hand and exclaimed, 'Oh, what idiots we have all been! Oh but this is wonderful! This is just as it must be!'"

They spoke for only a few minutes, but Bohr immediately agreed with everything that Meitner and Frisch had concluded. He said that he was astonished no one had thought of it sooner. Bohr was traveling to the United States onboard the ship *Drottningholm* with his 19-year-old son Erik and Leon Rosenfeld, a 33-year-old professor from the University of Liège. Bohr was so excited about working through various calculations involving fission that he had a blackboard installed in his cabin on the ship so that he and Rosenfeld could work on the problem as they traveled.

Frisch had asked Bohr to keep quiet about the discovery until he and Meitner had the chance to publish a report of their theory. He knew that Meitner would not receive credit for her work if she did not publish a paper about it right away. Bohr agreed, but he became so enthusiastic about the possibilities of fission that he found it difficult not to share the news. He apparently did not intend to undermine Meitner and Frisch, but once he had told other people, he could no longer control the information and how it spread. Soon after the boat docked at the 57th Street Pier in New York City, the gossip about fission had spread among the scientific community in the United States.

By the beginning of January, Meitner and Frisch's article should have been ready to mail, but Frisch wanted to do a few more follow-up experiments that Meitner had recommended to confirm their findings. Meitner had complained that she didn't have any decent laboratory equipment to work with, so Frisch decided to do some studies of his own when he got home. Frisch kept working, and on January 13, he directly observed pulses of energy, confirming that uranium atoms did release energy when split, just as he had predicted. He consulted with Meitner by phone, and then quickly wrote a 500-word article that summarized this experiment. He went to bed at 3 A.M., only to wake up four hours later when someone knocked at the door. A postman delivered a telegram stating that Frisch's father had been released from the concentration camp at Dachau, and that his parents would be immigrating to Sweden. Frisch was overjoyed and relieved.

On January 16, Frisch finally submitted two articles to the weekly scientific journal *Nature*, "A New Type of Nuclear Reaction" written by Meitner and Frisch, and "Physical Evidence for the Division of Heavy Nuclei under Neutron Bombardment" written by Frisch alone. In the cover letter, he did not point out that these articles were of extreme importance and should be published as soon as possible. The staff at *Nature* received the articles on January 17, but without any sense of their significance, the editors did not find room for publication until February 11, three weeks after they were submitted. This publication delay caused a great deal of controversy over who should receive credit for the discoveries, because other scientists know about the discovery before Meitner and Frisch published their findings.

The Formal Announcement

Bohr and Rosenfeld arrived in the United States on January 16, weeks before the Meitner-Frisch papers were published. Throughout their journey, Bohr and Rosenfeld had worked on the fission issue, and by the time they arrived in New York they both had a solid theoretical understanding of the process. Italian physicist Enrico Fermi and Hungarian physicist Leó Szilárd met Bohr's ship in New York. Rosenfeld didn't realize that the news about fission was a secret, so he immediately began to tell his colleagues everything he knew about the process.

On January 22 Frisch wrote a letter to Bohr saying that he was "currently planning various new experiments on these 'fission' processes." This was the first time the word "fission" had been used to describe splitting or dividing the atom. Frisch had come up with the term after hearing a biochemist friend use the word to describe the way living cells divided. The term perfectly described the division of the atom, too; it has been used ever since.

News of fission was officially announced to the physics world on January 26. Bohr and Fermi got up at the Fifth Conference on Theoretical Physics at the Carnegie Institute in Washington, D.C., and announced the discovery of fission, crediting Hahn and Strassmann for conducting the experiment and Meitner and Frisch for interpreting the results. The room was immediately thrown into chaos. Some scientists in attendance left the conference and rushed back to their laboratories to confirm Frisch's work or to start experiments of their own.

The implications of the research were immediate and far-reaching. International tensions were high and war seemed imminent. Because fission resulted in the release of enormous amount of energy, many scientists understood that this new discovery would very likely be used to create the ultimate weapon, the atomic bomb.

Credit Where Credit Is Due

Bohr tried to make sure that Meitner and Frisch got credit for their work, but it was difficult to recognize their research when it had not yet been published. On the night the news of fission was announced before the American Physical Society, Bohr wrote to his wife: "I was immediately frightened, as I had promised Frisch I would wait [to share the news] until Hahn's note was published and his [Frisch's] own was sent off." Bohr knew that at this point it would be hard—if not impossible—to ensure that Meitner and Frisch were given the recognition they deserved.

On February 3, Bohr wrote to Frisch:

I need not say how extremely delighted I am by your most important discovery, on which I congratulate you most heartily. . . . The experiments of Hahn, together with your aunt's and your explanation, have indeed raised quite a sensation not only among physicists, but in the daily press in America. Indeed, as you may have gathered from my telegrams and perhaps even, as I feared, from the Scandinavian press, there has been a rush in a number of American laboratories to compete in exploring the new field. On the last day of the conference in Washington, D.C., where Rosenfeld and I were present, the first results of detection of high energy splitters were already reported from various sides. Unaware as I was, to my great regret, of your own discovery, and not in possession even of the final text of your and your aunt's note to *Nature*, I could only stress (which I did most energetically) to all concerned that no public account of any such results could legitimately appear without mentioning your and your aunt's original interpretation of Hahn's results.

Bohr's concern was not misplaced. Meitner's name was rarely mentioned in the press accounts. An article in *Time* magazine stated:

"Last week the Hahn report reached the United States, and physicists sprang to their laboratories to see whether they could confirm it. Early this week, the laboratories of Columbia, Johns Hopkins, and the Carnegie Institution announced confirmation." Meitner and Frisch were not credited.

By late February, when the Meitner-Frisch articles in *Nature* were finally published, people had already read about Hahn's discovery of fission. Just as Bohr had feared, Meitner and Frisch were basically forgotten. The story of the discovery of fission and atomic energy was told without acknowledging Meitner's decades of work in the field or her paradigm-changing moment of understanding the process of fission. In addition, Frisch's contributions to proving the phenomenon were largely ignored, even though he was the first person to experimentally confirm what Hahn had discovered indirectly.

In time, Hahn himself helped to rewrite the history of the discovery of fission. At first, Hahn stressed that the discovery of fission had been the "work [of] the three of us." In a matter of weeks, Hahn turned his back on Meitner and excluded her from "his discovery." Fearing his own professional status and that of Strassmann, Hahn began to separate himself from Meitner and revise the history of their work together. He seemed to forget that he had begged Meitner for help, asking for her to explain his results. He began to discount and devalue her contributions to his research, ultimately claiming that the discovery of fission "owed nothing to physics"!

Meitner wrote to Hahn on March 10, 1939, insisting on proper credit. She reminded Hahn that "you and Strassmann" could not have made the important and "beautiful discovery" if "*we* had not done" research as a team with earlier uranium experiments. Their experiment was the culmination of years of work that came before.

Most other scientists working on transuranic research were annoyed with themselves when they read about Meitner's results: Once fission was explained, it seemed glaringly apparent. Even though she was not prone to profanity, when Irène Curie read Hahn and

Strassmann's article about the discovery of fission, she said: "Oh, what dumb asses we have been!"

Once again, Irène had come close to making another important discovery, but she missed it. Like Hahn, Irène had come to the point where she identified evidence that contradicted the known rules of physics, but she couldn't figure out which rules were wrong. Irène wondered whether she and Frédéric would have been able to beat Meitner to the discovery if they had been working together. This missed opportunity may have been even more bitter for Irène because Meitner—her rival in the search for transuranics—had been the one to beat her.

Ida Noddack's Claim

In March 1939, German physicist Ida Noddack claimed that she had discovered fission five years before Hahn's article appeared. Hahn wrote to Meitner:

> Another not very pleasant situation is a letter to *Naturwis-senschaften* by Ida Noddack, in which she accuses me of not citing her, after she predicted already in 1934 that uranium splits into lighter nuclei. I'm sure you remember her article. . . . She mocks what Strassmann and I have done: We always retracted and changed, etc.

In Meitner's response, she called Noddack's article meaningless and said she didn't remember much about it.

Noddack's article about uranium splitting appeared in the German journal *Angewandte Chemie* in September 1934, but it was never taken seriously. In the piece Noddack suggested that the unexpected findings in transuranic experiments could be explained by the uranium nucleus splitting into two mid-sized pieces. She speculated that "one can imagine that when heavy nuclei are bombarded with neutrons, these nuclei break apart into several large fragments, which are indeed isotopes of known elements but not neighbors of the irradiated elements." Both the article and her hypothesis were ignored by almost everyone, including Meitner and the Joliot-Curies. The theory defied all previous experience of physics, and Noddack offered no empirical proof to support it. Although Noddack was now ready to take credit for the theory, neither she nor anyone else seemed to take the argument seriously enough to perform the simple experiment needed to prove her theory. At the time, the theory seemed too farfetched to be worthy of discussion or experimental exploration.

German physicist and chemist Ida Noddack (1896–1978) mentioned the idea of nuclear fission in a 1934 article, but she never researched the idea. She and her husband, Walter Noddack, discovered element 75, rhenium.

Hahn and Strassmann wanted to publish an angry response to Noddack's accusations, but the editor of *Naturwissenschaften* convinced them not to. Instead, a note appeared in the journal: "The gentlemen Otto Hahn and Fritz Strassmann inform us that they have neither the time nor the desire to answer. . . . They want their colleagues to be the judges of the correctness of Frau Ida Noddack's demands and the manner or her presentation." Meitner told Hahn: "Nothing could better illustrate her unscientific smallmindedness and envy than her own words. She really has made a great fool of herself."

The controversy surrounding Noddack's claim strengthened Hahn's opinion that he and Strassmann—and no one else, including Meitner—should receive credit for the discovery of fission. He wouldn't honor Noddack with so much as a footnote. From that point on, he became more entrenched in his belief that Meitner not only did not deserve credit for the discovery, but also that she had inhibited his progress as long as she was working with him in Berlin.

The "Fission Bomb"

Reports on the discovery of fission jolted the scientific community into action. In the spring and summer of 1938, dozens of articles on fission appeared in various scientific journals. Scientists immediately understood that fission could be used to design a weapon far more lethal that anything previously imagined. In a military conflict, the side to first develop a working fission bomb would be at a distinct advantage in war. This was more than a theoretical threat: Germany had already annexed Austria and had mobilized its military.

At that time, scientists published their research openly, sharing their data with the goal of perpetuating knowledge. With the discovery of fission—especially during wartime—some scientists believed that it was in the national interest to clamp down on information sharing so that it would become more difficult for the enemy in general—and Germany in particular—to develop what was first called a "fission bomb."

Hungarian physicist Leó Szilárd was the scientist who worried that Germany might develop a bomb that could be used against the United States and other Allied countries. He and Bohr favored international cooperation and control of the discovery, to ultimately result in an international demonstration of the bomb's explosive power without the need to ever use it in combat.

He also believed that scientists should stop publishing articles about fission and the potential for a nuclear chain reaction. Szilárd understood that German scientists would be working on making a bomb; why would other scientists want to share their information with the enemy? With that in mind, in February 1939, Szilárd wrote the Joliot-Curies:

I personally feel that these things should be discussed privately among the physicists of England, France, and America; and that there should be no publication on this topic if it should turn out that neutrons are, in fact, emitted, and that a chain reaction might be possible.

Szilárd and other experts contacted leading scientific journals and pleaded with them not to publish articles relating to fission or a chain reaction. Some scientists agreed with Szilárd and immediately stopped publishing their work. Others, including the Joliot-Curies, believed that any form of censorship—including self-censorship—ran against their core beliefs of internationalism and freedom of science. The Joliot-Curies refused to stop publishing, arguing that scientific discoveries should not be owned by individuals, patented for profit, or used as military intelligence.

International relations were further strained when Hitler invaded Czechoslovakia on March 16, 1939. Szilárd again contacted Irène and Frédéric and urged them to delay publishing results of future fission experiments in light of their possible military use. The Joliot-Curies didn't believe that it would be possible to build a bomb fast enough to make a difference in the war and, even if it were possible, they thought it would be impossible to stop leaks to Nazi scientists whether information was published or not. In addition, on a philosophical level, Irène and Frédéric said that if scientists in Allied countries stopped publishing their research, they would have already allowed Hitler to win by restricting their freedom of speech.

After careful consideration, on April 7, the Joliot-Curies sent Szilárd a one-word response: "No." On the same day, Frédéric sent *Nature* the results of experiments and calculations he and Irène had done that estimated the number of neutrons emitted per fission; the article was published on April 22, 1939. This was the first article to show that fission could produce enough neutrons to trigger a chain reaction.

Irène and Frédéric did not realize it at the time, but Szilárd's concerns were well founded.

By April 1939, the German government had formed a secret committee to discuss ways to use the fission of uranium for military purposes. (Although he did not approve of the politics of Hitler or the Nazi Party, Hahn was one of the senior members of the group because he knew more about fission than any other German physicist.) Irène and Frédéric never intended to help the Germans; they simply wanted to continue their research on fission with the goal of creating a nuclear reactor that could supply a reliable source of energy for the benefit of all. They were naïve in their belief that scientists could stand together in opposing the use of nuclear fission to create weapons of mass destruction.

While the Joliot-Curies had not patented their work before, in this situation Frédéric was convinced by three of his colleagues—Hans von Halban from Austria, Francis Perrin from France, and Lew Kowarsk from Russia—to apply for French patents on several inventions employing fission, including a nuclear reactor, a regulator, and a potential nuclear bomb. (The applications were not granted until 1950, after the war.)

The Joliot-Curies stubbornly refused to stop sharing their work. In time, the French team would change their approach, Szilárd reasoned. He said: "If *we* persisted in *not* publishing, Joliot would have to come around; otherwise, he would be at a disadvantage because we could know *his* results and yet, he would *not* know ours."

Szilárd, Einstein, and Roosevelt

While Szilárd was not successful in silencing the Joliot-Curies, he decided that he would try to get the United States government involved in coordinating a fission-bomb program. Szilárd and another scientist drove to the Institute for Advanced Study in Princeton, New Jersey, to meet with Albert Einstein, who had left Germany

and immigrated to the United States in 1933. They learned that
Einstein was on vacation, so they tracked him down at his retreat on
Long Island, New York.

When Szilárd explained his concern about fission being used to
create an atomic bomb, Einstein expressed surprise. "I never thought
of that!" Einstein said.

The famous letter drafted by Szilárd and signed by Einstein
is widely considered to be the catalyst that compelled President
Franklin Roosevelt to consider the possibilities of a German nuclear
threat. The letter reads, in part:

> August 2, 1939
>
> Sir:
>
> Some recent work by E. Fermi and L. Szilárd, which has
> been communicated to me in manuscript, leads me to
> expect that the element uranium may be turned into a
> new and important source of energy in the immediate
> future. . . . In the course of the last four months it has been
> made probable—through the work of Joliot in France as
> well as Fermi and Szilárd in America—that it may become
> possible to set up a nuclear chain reaction in a large mass of
> uranium by which vast amounts of power and large quanti-
> ties of new radium-like elements would be generated. Now
> it appears almost certain that this could be achieved in the
> immediate future.

This new phenomenon would also lead to the construction of
bombs. . . . Einstein grasped the gravity of the situation; he said he
wanted the United States to make the bomb before Hitler did.

The president needed to take action as soon as possible. One
month later, on September 1, 1939, Germany invaded Poland. On
September 3, England declared war on Germany, and France followed five hours later. World War II had begun.

Albert Einstein
Old Grove Rd.
Nassau Point
Peconic, Long Island

August 2nd, 1939

F.D. Roosevelt,
President of the United States,
White House
Washington, D.C.

Sir:

    Some recent work by E.Fermi and L. Szilard, which has been com-
municated to me in manuscript, leads me to expect that the element uranium may be turned into a new and important source of energy in the immediate future. Certain aspects of the situation which has arisen seem
to call for watchfulness and, if necessary, quick action on the part
of the Administration. I believe therefore that it is my duty to bring
to your attention the following facts and recommendations:

    In the course of the last four months it has been made probable -
through the work of Joliot in France as well as Fermi and Szilard in
America - that it may become possible to set up a nuclear chain reaction
in a large mass of uranium,by which vast amounts of power and large quantities of new radium-like elements would be generated. Now it appears
almost certain that this could be achieved in the immediate future.

    This new phenomenon would also lead to the construction of bombs,
and it is conceivable - though much less certain - that extremely powerful bombs of a new type may thus be constructed. A single bomb of this
type, carried by boat and exploded in a port, might very well destroy
the whole port together with some of the surrounding territory. However,
such bombs might very well prove to be too heavy for transportation by
air.

A copy of the letter Albert Einstein sent to President Franklin D. Roosevelt on August 2, 1939.

On Oct. 19, 1939, the president responded to Einstein's letter. He wrote:

My dear Professor:

I want to thank you for your recent letter and the most interesting and important enclosure. I found this data of such import that I have convened a board consisting of the head

-2-

The United States has only very poor ores of uranium in moderate quantities. There is some good ore in Canada and the former Czechoslovakia, while the most important source of uranium is Belgian Congo.

In view of this situation you may think it desirable to have some permanent contact maintained between the Administration and the group of physicists working on chain reactions in America. One possible way of achieving this might be for you to entrust with this task a person who has your confidence and who could perhaps serve in an inofficial capacity. His task might comprise the following:

a) to approach Government Departments, keep them informed of the further development, and put forward recommendations for Government action, giving particular attention to the problem of securing a supply of uranium ore for the United States;

b) to speed up the experimental work,which is at present being carried on within the limits of the budgets of University laboratories, by providing funds, if such funds be required, through his contacts with private persons who are willing to make contributions for this cause, and perhaps also by obtaining the co-operation of industrial laboratories which have the necessary equipment.

I understand that Germany has actually stopped the sale of uranium from the Czechoslovakian mines which she has taken over. That she should have taken such early action might perhaps be understood on the ground that the son of the German Under-Secretary of State, von Weizsäcker, is attached to the Kaiser-Wilhelm-Institut in Berlin where some of the American work on uranium is now being repeated.

Yours very truly,

A. Einstein

(Albert Einstein)

of the Bureau of Standards and chosen representatives of the Army and Navy to thoroughly investigate the possibilities of your suggestion regarding the element uranium. . . .

This letter marked the beginning of the U.S. atomic research program. The race was on: The world was at war and the winning side would likely be the one that first figured out how to build an atomic bomb.

13

WAR

URING MOST OF the war years, Irène Joliot-
Curie's tuberculosis forced her to leave her
work and spend time convalescing at a
sanatorium in Switzerland. Frédéric Joliot-Curie, on the other hand,
continued his research in France while at the same time becoming
more involved in politics.

Shortly after France declared war, Frédéric was named a captain
in the French artillery reserves with responsibility for coordinating
government research. Two coworkers who had assisted Frédéric with
his fission research—Lew Kowarski and Hans von Halban—became
naturalized French citizens so that they could join the military and
continue to work with Frédéric.

At first, the team planned to continue their work on fission with
the goal of creating a nuclear power plant—what Frédéric called a
"uranium boiler"—using slow neutrons to create a sustained chain
reaction of uranium. Frédéric had only a theoretical interest in developing a bomb; his real goal was to develop a safe and inexpensive
source of nuclear energy. According to the Associated Press, Frédéric
was trying "to find a way to make a $2 pound of uranium produce
enough energy as was obtained by burning $10,000 worth of coal."

While this was a new area of research, many people felt confident that, in time, Frédéric would be able to do it, and Irène was eager to make suggestions whenever she could.

For his work, Frédéric needed a supply of heavy water (water enriched by the isotope deuterium and used to slow down the chain reaction during nuclear fission). Many of the hydrogen atoms in heavy water—$2H_2O$—contain neutrons, making them heavier and denser than those found in ordinary water. Heavy water was hard to come by and quite expensive; the only source in Europe was Norsk Hydro in Norway, which collected the heavy water generated as a byproduct of creating synthetic ammonia.

Researchers all over the world had by this time realized the importance of heavy water in research on nuclear fission, whether for energy or for bomb-making. German company IG Farben owned 25 percent of the Norwegian water company, and it ordered that all of the heavy water be sent to Germany for research.

The head of the Norwegian company recognized the political and military realities of the day: The country with the heavy water had a distinct advantage in the race to produce a nuclear bomb. The company tried to stall the order, but it was not going to be able to hold out much longer. Now a French military officer with scientific responsibility, Frédéric had to come up with a plan to get his hands on the water before the Germans did.

In February 1940, a French lieutenant traveling under his mother's maiden name flew to Amsterdam with a bank note for 36 million French francs, approximately $1.4 million. His mission was to get to Norway and bring back the entire stock of heavy water to France or, if that was impossible, to destroy it by contaminating it with a small vial of cadmium that Frédéric had given him for that purpose.

When the lieutenant left France, the German military became suspicious and ordered his capture and arrest. Somehow, the officer made his way to Sweden and then Norway undetected by the Nazis.

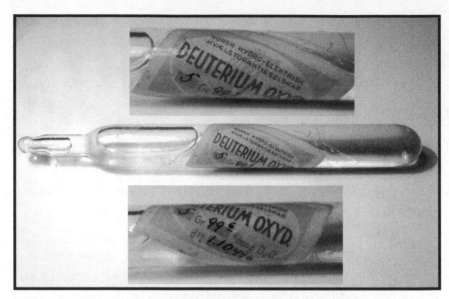

The heavy water produced by Norsk Hydro was stored in glass vials, which the French smuggled out of Amsterdam during World War II.

When he finally met with Norsk Hydro, the company executive agreed to lend France its entire stockpile of heavy water—185 kilograms or 408 pounds—for use until the end of the war.

The next challenge: Getting the water back to France. At the plant, the heavy water was sealed into 26 seven-liter cans. On March 12, the cans were loaded into a taxi and taken to the airport as part of a carefully orchestrated scheme. When the taxi arrived, two planes on scheduled flights waited on the runway: one flight was to Amsterdam, the other to Perth, Scotland. The French lieutenant casually boarded the flight for Amsterdam, ignoring the other plane. A few minutes before takeoff, the taxi carrying the heavy water rushed out onto the airfield and a French officer got out of the car, making a scene about being late to board the plane to Amsterdam.

During the commotion on the tarmac, the planes were out of sight of the terminal and the heavy water was secured onboard the plane to Scotland; the lieutenant switched planes as well.

Both planes took off moments later. The flight to Scotland went uninterrupted; the flight to Amsterdam was forced down by the German military, who searched the plane for unusual cargo but found nothing.

In a much less dramatic chain of events, the heavy water was moved again from Scotland to Paris, where it was stored in the vaults at the Collège de France. Frédéric realized that the water wasn't safe in Paris, either, so it was moved several times again, at one point being stored in a death-row cell of a prison in Riom, France. Once the Germans invaded France and Paris fell, the water was secretly evacuated to England aboard the ship *Broompark*. This time, Frédéric's coworkers von Halban and Kowarski drove the water to the ship and secured it inside the life rafts; the hope was that the heavy water could be rescued if the ship was torpedoed en route. Once the cargo arrived in England, it was stored temporarily at another state prison, and at one point it spent time in the custody of the royal librarian at Windsor Castle.

Most importantly, the heavy water was out of German hands. Without the heavy water, the Germans would be limited in their nuclear research, at least for a while. When the occupying Germans questioned Frédéric about what had happened to the heavy water, he told them that it had been on board another ship that had been sunk on its journey to England. They had no evidence to contradict Frédéric, so they believed him.

Fermi's Chain Reaction

Hiding heavy water from the Germans wasn't enough. In order to develop an Allied bomb, researchers had to figure out how to create sustained fission using an ongoing chain reaction. What the fission experiments had proved in theory would need to be performed on a much larger scale in order to make a bomb, or a nuclear energy

Enrico Fermi, 1943. Italian physicist Fermi (1901–1954) is best known for his work on the first nuclear reactor (Chicago Pile-1). He is often referred to as "the father of the atomic bomb."

plant, for that matter. In other words, the next step would be to design an experiment that showed that one uranium atom could split and release neutrons that would in turn split other atoms and so forth, in a self-sustaining series so that the fission process would continue.

Some physicists thought that a chain reaction was impossible. Others thought it was theoretically possible, but that researchers would be unable to find enough of the special form of uranium— isotope U-235—that was required for the reaction. More than 99 percent of the uranium found in nature is U-238—a form with 146 neutrons—but the type required for nuclear fission was the less common U-235 form, which has 143 neutrons. The big difference to researchers is that U-235 is the only naturally occurring isotope that can divide through fission in a sustained chain reaction.

At the request of the United States government, Italian physicist Enrico Fermi, who had immigrated to the United States in 1938, came to the University of Chicago to do his research. He set up a laboratory deep underground in the university's squash courts, and he built an enormous lead-shielded "pile" to test whether he could create a self-sustaining chain reaction involving the fission of U-235 isotopes.

On December 2, 1942—four years after Meitner and Frisch announced their discovery of fission—the first nuclear chain reaction took place. The test involved a massive uranium core crossed by neutron-absorbing cadmium rods. One by one, the control rods of cadmium were pulled out, allowing the reaction to begin. When the final cadmium rod, which had been nicknamed "Zip," was removed, the chain reaction became self-sustaining. At that point, the U-235 was dividing and emitting neutrons fast enough to create an on-going reaction. Twenty-eight minutes later, "Zip" was slipped back into position and the reaction slowed and was brought back under control.

The success of this experiment showed that an atomic bomb might be feasible. By 1943, a large-scale, top-secret operation in Los Alamos, New Mexico called the Manhattan Project was working to create an atomic weapon. Other Allied nations joined forces with the effort in the hope that by working together, they could develop a bomb before Germany did. It was no longer a competition for recognition or status in scientific circles; the side that won the arms race would very likely win the war.

A drawing of the first nuclear reactor, built in 1942 at the University of Chicago, where scientists created the first self-sustaining nuclear chain reaction.

The Joliot-Curies During the War

While Frédéric and Irène Joliot-Curie had always been open about sharing their research findings without censorship, when France went to war with Germany they realized that they should no longer share all of their work on fission. Frédéric had been fascinated by fission since the first time he read about Meitner's discovery. He saw it as a possible solution to France's energy problems. In 1939, France imported nearly all of its oil and a third of its coal from other countries. If it developed nuclear power, France could become energy independent.

Irène and Frédéric didn't initially believe that a bomb could be developed in time to make a difference in the war with Germany, but they knew that other countries could try to adapt their research to wartime applications. On October 30, 1939, they placed their documentation on nuclear fission and nuclear reactors in a sealed envelope and stored it in a safe at the Academy of Sciences. The envelope would remain unopened for the next ten years.

The Joliot-Curies' worries about protecting their research became an even greater concern in June 1940, when Germans marched into Paris. Ultimately, France was split into two zones: the German-occupied zone—more than half the country, including Paris—and unoccupied France in the South. A Nazi loyalist took charge of Frédéric's laboratory, and four Nazi scientists were assigned to work under him.

Irène was preoccupied with convalescence to treat her tuberculosis. Frédéric tried to cooperate with the Nazis enough to keep his laboratory up and running, but not so much that he supported the German cause. Some colleagues accused him of being on the Nazi side; others considered him a practical person who was trying to figure out a way to get by during impossible times. Frédéric had to be cautious about the work he did in the lab, trying to appear busy but not completing work that could support the Nazis in the development of a bomb. Instead of working on fission, Frédéric and his team turned to biological research, conducting experiments involving the use of radioactive iodine to assess thyroid function.

Frédéric remained loyal to France, but his politics were becoming more radical. In 1942, the German Gestapo, or secret police, killed several of Frédéric's close friends—including Paul Langevin's son-in law—and in response Joliot joined the Communist Party. "I became a communist because I am a patriot," Frédéric said. It was a dangerous decision, because the Germans were known to execute communists.

As Irène watched fascist governments gain power throughout Europe, she became more politically active as well. She supported civil and political equality for women, including freedom for women to work in the sciences. She opposed fascist governments that promoted dictators with absolute power, who controlled industry, suppressed opposition, and promoted aggressive nationalism and racism.

Irène joined the Popular Front—a coalition of moderates, socialists, and communists dedicated to resisting fascism—and she was asked to serve as undersecretary of state for scientific research. She took the job, calling it "a sacrifice for the feminist cause in France." She wanted to advance "the most precious right of women . . . to exercise under the same conditions as men the profession for which they're qualified by education and experience." She was asked to serve as one of the first female cabinet ministers in France: She accepted, although ironically, she could not vote in a public election because women did not gain suffrage in France until 1945. At the time she accepted the post, she planned to serve only three months and then resign and surrender her seat to a friend so that she could focus her efforts on her research.

Irène lacked political skills; diplomacy and tact were never her style. When invited to an event or meeting, she would respond with a simple yes or no, without embellishing her remarks with the traditional flowery language often used in French business letters. Her secretary tried to draft letters stating that she was "desolate" to miss a meeting or she sent her "profound respects" or "deepest tribute" to a colleague, but Irène deleted the unnecessary and exaggerated language, leaving the basic message. She also hated wasting time. When meetings dragged on or lost her interest, she got up and left.

Over the years, Irène joined several women's rights organizations, including the French Women's Union. She said: "I am not one of those . . . who think that a woman [scientist] . . . can disinterest herself from her role as a woman, either in private or public life."

Wartime Heroics

During the war, Irène's health became much worse. Food and fuel shortages caused her tuberculosis to recur. Her face developed deep wrinkles—she looked much older than a woman in her forties— and she suffered from chronic fatigue. Doctors told her to work in moderation, but she found it difficult to do. Instead, she had a cot brought to her office at the Curie Institute, so that she could lie down in the afternoon but still continue with her research. The fatigue was debilitating at times; while traveling she once became so exhausted that she had to lie on the floor in a public place and take a nap while others kept walking around her. Since there was little that could be done for her, Irène's solution was to avoid discussing her health, even with her closest family members. Still, throughout the war she spent several weeks or months each year at sanatoriums, typically in the Alps.

Toward the end of the war, Frédéric arranged for Irène and the children to leave France, but Irène refused to leave the country until her daughter, Hélène, completed her baccalaureate examinations. Hélène took the exams secretly in a small border village, and on June 6, 1944, Irène and her two children hiked over the Jura

Mountains into Switzerland. Irène was carrying a heavy physics volume in her knapsack, as well as her logarithm tables with "Radium Institute" inscribed in the margins. They were lucky: June 6 was D-Day, the day the Americans invaded the beaches of Normandy, France; German border security was distracted, making their escape a bit easier.

Once his family was secure, Frédéric went underground in the French Resistance movement. He used the pseudonym "Jean-Pierre Gaumont," and when he wrote letters to Irène, he referred to her using the pseudonym "Gabrielle." For a while, Frédéric moved every day, never sleeping in the same place twice. He met other agents on the banks of the Seine near Notre Dame, posing as a fisherman but passing along formulas for explosives and instructions on how to make homemade grenades.

At that time, the Allied forces had arrived in Normandy and were working their way toward Paris. In the meantime, Frédéric and other Resistance members were working to prepare for the inevitable uprising. On August 19, 1944, Frédéric carried two suitcases loaded with the chemicals necessary to make Molotov cocktails into the police building in Paris. The Parisians were called to arms, ready to strike down the German forces. Frédéric and two assistants worked in a makeshift laboratory in the basement, pouring out bottles of champagne onto the floor and refilling the bottles with the combination of gasoline and acid necessary to make the explosive devices. The bottles were wrapped with paper that had been soaked in potassium chlorate, an explosive agent, and then they were carried to the upper floors where they could be lobbed out of the windows in the direction of the German tanks surrounding the building.

Several tanks were destroyed using the makeshift weapons, and the Germans ultimately retreated, at least for the time being. Frédéric and the others churned out the simple explosives to defend themselves for days as the fighting continued.

The Allies reached Paris by August 25, and the city was liberated at last. Frédéric became a war hero, becoming a commander of the Legion of Honor, the highest decoration in France, as well as a recipient of the Croix de Guerre, with palms—the Cross of War—for heroic deeds in combat that were recognized in an army dispatch.

"I will have nothing to do with the bomb!"

During the war years, the United States government invited Lise Meitner to participate in the Manhattan Project, but she refused. "I will have nothing to do with the bomb!" she said. Meitner remembered what she had witnessed on the battlefields of World War I, and she wanted no part of that kind of destruction. Meitner worried about how the war was affecting friends and family left back in Germany and in German-occupied Austria. Hahn's son—Hanno, Meitner's godson—lost an arm fighting in the German army. Max Planck's home was destroyed, and his son was killed by the Nazis for his part in an attempt to assassinate Hitler. Dirk Coster and his wife were starving in German-occupied Holland.

Meitner continued to work, but she was frustrated that she wasn't able to do many follow-up experiments on fission with the limited equipment available in her laboratory. She mentored a few doctoral students and developed creative new ways to construct experimental apparatus for her lab. She continued to publish her research, which featured new theories on fission and investigations of gamma rays.

Meitner lost touch with Hahn during much of the war. He and nine other German scientists had been captured and taken to a country estate known as Farm Hall in England. The Allies did not want to put these esteemed scientists in jail, but they did not want them to have a chance to further their research on a bomb. The estate had been wired with secret microphones so that the Allies could eavesdrop on their every conversation to find out how far the Germans

Prisoners at a concentration camp in Ebensee, Austria, 1945. The camp was a sub-camp of a larger facility in Mauthausen.

had progressed toward building an atomic bomb. Hahn and the others were held there until the end of 1945 when the war ended.

One of the most horrific experiences of the war for Meitner was the realization of what had happened in the German concentration camps. As the war was winding down, Meitner saw thousands of concentration camp survivors as they traveled from the camps to Sweden. The gaunt faces and hollow stares haunted her.

The more Meitner learned about the horrors in Hitler's death camps, the more conflicted she felt about her time in Germany and her relationships with the people she knew there—especially Hahn. On June 27, 1945, Meitner wrote a heartfelt letter to Hahn. He later claimed that the letter never reached him, but a copy of its contents had been filed by his secretary and remained in the file for 40 years. Meitner wrote:

Dear Otto,

... I am writing in a great hurry, although I have so much
to say that's so close to my heart. Remember that, please,
and read the letter with the assurance of my unwavering
friendship.

In my mind I've written you many letters in the last months,
because it was clear to me that even people like you and Max
[von Laue, a German physicist] did not understand the real
situation [in Nazi Germany]. . . . That has been Germany's
misfortune: that all of you lost your standards of justice and
fairness. As early as March 1935, you told me that Horlein
[the treasurer of the group that sponsored the Kaiser Wilhelm Institute] had told you that horrible things would be
done to the Jews. He knew about all the crimes that had
been planned and that would later be carried out; in spite
of that he was a member of the Party and you still regarded
him—in spite of it—as a very respectable man, and let him
guide you in your behavior toward your best friend [refer-
ring to herself].

All of you also worked for Nazi Germany, and never even at-
tempted passive resistance. Of course, to save your troubled
consciences, you occasionally helped an oppressed person;
still, you let millions of innocent people be murdered, and
there was never a sound of protest.

I must write you this because so much of what happens to
you and the Third Reich now depends upon your recognizing what all of you allowed to happen. Long before the end
of the war, people here in neutral Sweden were discussing
what ought to be done with German scholars at the end of

the war . . . namely that you know you bear a responsibility for the occurrences as a result of your passiveness, and that you feel it is necessary to help out in making reparations for the occurrences as far as that is even possible. Many, though, believe that it is already too late for that. They say that you all betrayed your friends at the outset, then your men and children by allowing them to risk their lives in a criminal war, and that finally, you betrayed Germany itself: when the war was totally hopeless, you didn't even oppose the senseless destruction of Germany. That sounds pitiless, but yet believe me, it is the truest friendship that makes me write you all this. You really can't expect the world to pity Germany. What we have heard recently about the unfathomable atrocities of the concentration camps exceeds everything we had feared. . . .

Perhaps you remember that when I was still in Germany (and I know today that it was not only stupid, but a great injustice that I didn't leave immediately), I often said to you, "As long as just we [the Jewish people] and not you have sleepless nights, it won't get any better in Germany." But you never had any sleepless nights: you didn't want to see—it was too disturbing.

Meitner no doubt felt enormous relief when she mailed the letter. She had, at last, expressed her deepest emotions about the war and her feelings of betrayal. She had been brave enough to take a stand and to state her beliefs, well aware of the possible consequences. She could no longer be silent: She had witnessed what had happened when people refused to take a stand against evil. The war had changed the quiet, subservient woman Meitner had been when she first met Hahn. She had—at last—discovered her voice.

August 6, 1945

While Germany had surrendered to the Allied forces in May 1945, the fighting continued in the Pacific against Japan. Meitner was staying with friends at a lakeside cottage in central Sweden when she heard the news: At 8:15 A.M. on August 6, 1945, the American B-29 bomber, *Enola Gay*, dropped "Little Boy," a four-ton atomic bomb, over Hiroshima, Japan. It detonated with the explosive power of 16,000 tons of TNT, flattening the city and killing thousands of people. Within months, as many as 160,000 people would be dead, either as a direct result of the bomb or from the insidious side effects of radiation exposure and poisoning.

Stunned, Meitner and her friend sat in silence, trying to understand the magnitude of the destruction. The bomb had employed the fission of uranium in a chain reaction to create a massive explosion, just as Meitner had predicted.

The silence was interrupted by a knock at the door. The cottage did not have a telephone, so a neighbor had run over to tell Meitner that a local newspaper wanted to interview her. Not long afterward, a reporter arrived and asked Meitner about her work on the atomic bomb. She told him that she had *never* worked on any nuclear weapons project. She had worked on various physics projects, but she had never intended for her work to be used to create a bomb. Never.

More reporters approached Meitner trying to get the opinions of the scientist who played such a vital role in unleashing the power that lurked within the atom. They were intrigued by the idea that fission had been discovered by a female German scientist who had fled Nazi Germany. Overnight, Meitner, a shy and quiet scientist, became world famous.

Three days later, First Lady Eleanor Roosevelt asked to interview Meitner for an NBC trans-Atlantic radio broadcast. The arrangements were made for a long-distance connection between the Swedish countryside and Washington, D.C. The interview took place on

At the time this photo was taken, smoke billowed 20,000 feet above Hiroshima, Japan.

August 9, the same day that a second atomic bomb was dropped on Japan, this time on Nagasaki. In this historic conversation, Mrs. Roosevelt congratulated Meitner on her major contribution in interpreting the process of nuclear fission, and compared her to Marie Curie. She also invited Meitner to someday visit the United States.

During the interview, both Meitner and Roosevelt expressed their belief in the need for world cooperation in politics and science.

Meitner also called for greater involvement of women in the creation of a lasting peace and for the responsible use of nuclear power. Meitner said that she was surprised that her work on fission had been turned into a weapon so quickly. Her position on the bomb was clear. She said: "It is an unfortunate accident that this discovery (of fission) came about in time of war."

As a woman, Meitner felt that she had an additional duty to try to avoid war. She said: "Women have a great responsibility and they are obligated to try, so far as they can, to prevent another war. I hope that the construction of the atom bomb not only will help to finish this awful war, but that we will be able to also use this great energy that has been released for peaceful work."

Meitner was right. The lethal power demonstrated by the bomb stunned the Japanese, who surrendered unconditionally on September 2, 1945. World War II had ended at last.

Although she did not seek publicity, Meitner became a scientific celebrity. Hahn became jealous of the press attention that Meitner was getting for discovering fission. He issued a press release a few days after the bomb was dropped. It stated:

> As long as Professor Meitner was in Germany, there was no discussion of the fission of uranium. It was considered impossible. Based on extensive chemical investigations of the chemical elements caused by irradiating uranium with neurons, Hahn and Strassmann were forced to assume at the end of 1938 that uranium splits into two parts. . . ."

Hahn was very eager to ensure his place in history as the one who discovered fission. This was Hahn's position and it did not change over the years.

Like Lise Meitner, Frédéric and Irène Joliot-Curie were horrified to learn about the detonation of the atomic bomb. Irène said that she was glad Marie Curie did not live long enough to see the day that an atomic bomb was used. In a lecture she presented after

Leó Szilárd. Albert Einstein. In 1946, Leó Szilárd and Albert Einstein founded the Emergency Committee of Atomic Scientists, a group dedicated to promoting peace and warning the public about the dangers of nuclear weapons. Half of the committee consisted of scientists who had worked on the Manhattan Project. Lise Meitner donated money to the group.

the war, she said: "It grieves us that a great country like the USA is squandering all its energies on augmenting the destructive power of atomic bombs while neglecting other major problems of universal interest."

The Joliot-Curies thought that the bomb was an abomination, a distortion, and an outright betrayal of the discoveries they had made and the beauty of the natural world. Frédéric wrote:

> The immense reserves of energy contained in the uranium devices can also be liberated slowly enough to be used practically for the benefit of mankind. I am personally convinced that atomic energy will be of inestimable service to mankind in peacetime.

Both the Joliot-Curies and Lise Meitner felt guilty about contributing to the creation of the atomic bomb. While they would never have participated in the making of a deadly weapon, the work of both Irène Curie and Lise Meitner played significant roles in its eventual development—Irène by creating artificial radioactivity and Meitner by unleashing the idea of fission. They also felt betrayed that their work had been appropriated for wartime purposes. They believed that science was pure and apolitical, almost divine in its absolute truth. Science did not answer to any political party or religion or nationality. Using the knowledge of fission to kill human beings was unfathomable, contrary to all that they believed. Neither one intended for their beloved science to be used for such destructive purposes, but they could not control what others did with their discoveries.

OVERLOOKED

On November 16, 1945, just three months after the bombings of Hiroshima and Nagasaki, the Royal Swedish Academy of Sciences announced that Otto Hahn had won the 1944 Nobel Prize in Chemistry "for his discovery of the fission of heavy nuclei." (The award was announced a year late and presented at the 1946 ceremony because of the war.) For months, Meitner had heard rumors that she was under consideration for either the physics or chemistry prize, but in the end her contributions to the discovery of fission were overlooked by the Nobel committee.

Hahn was being held at Farm Hall in England when he heard the news of his prize broadcast by the BBC. The other detainees toasted Hahn's success and, at least on that night, they were proud to be German.

In Sweden, Meitner's friends complained that she had been unjustly ignored because she was a woman and she was of Jewish ancestry. Meitner acknowledged to those closest to her that she felt cheated. After all, she had designed Hahn's experiments and interpreted the results, and Otto Robert Frisch had been the one to collaborate on the proof.

Farm Hall, the house in Godmanchester, England, where ten German scientists were held captive during the last part of World War II. The house was bugged so that the Allies could listen in and try to learn the details about any progress made by the German nuclear program.

The news that Meitner had been excluded surprised many scientists, and some openly disagreed with the decision. They did not object to recognizing Hahn's achievement, but they thought that Meitner—and Strassmann—should have been acknowledged, too. Strassmann, who had worked with Hahn and Meitner, said: "What does it matter that Lise Meitner did not take direct part in the 'discovery'. . . ? [She] was the intellectual leader of our team and therefore she was one of us, even if she was not actually present for the 'discovery of fission.'"

Birgit Broome Aminoff, a scientist and wife of a member of the Nobel Foundation, wrote to Meitner:

Long before the release of nuclear energy had been realized on a practical scale, it seemed to me that [you] had reached a status equivalent to that of many Nobel Prize recipients. It must therefore have been very bitter that for completely unrelated reasons you were forced to leave the laboratory where the now-rewarded discovery was so close, and thereby lost the possibility to complete a work which promised to be the natural climax of a long and devoted career as a scientist.

Meitner responded:

Surely Hahn fully deserved the Nobel Prize in chemistry. There is really no doubt about it. But I believe that Frisch and I contributed something not insignificant to the clarification of the process of uranium fission—how it originates and that it produces so much energy, and that was something very remote from Hahn. For this reason I found it a bit unjust that in the newspaper I was called a *Mitarbeiterin* [an assistant] of Hahn's in the same sense that Strassmann was. Your letter, therefore, was a double present; a warm understanding word can mean so much. A thousand thanks for it.

Several practical issues played into the decision of who was to receive the prize. For one thing, it was an interdisciplinary discovery, involving both chemistry and physics, which made it difficult for some scientists to allocate the contributions made by physicist Meitner and chemist Hahn. In addition, according to committee rules, the Nobel Prize could be awarded to no more than three people, and if Meitner were recognized, Frisch and Strassmann should be too, bringing the total number of recipients to four. After the award was announced, the committee received additional information about Meitner's contributions, but there was resistance to changing the award recipients at that time.

Physicist Wolfgang Pauli considered Meitner a victim of poor timing. He wrote:

In 1944, it was not officially known that nuclear fission was so important, and chemists were primarily interested in Hahn's work because he had disproved Fermi's Nobel Prize [for transuranic elements]. If fission had been known to be so important, if the prize had been given after the war, it would have been clear that Meitner had to be included. It always takes at least several years for a great experiment to be understood. The experiment happened in 1939; a lot of the work of fission done in France, England, and the United States was immediately classified, and so its importance wasn't generally understood. She should have had the prize in physics the same years that Hahn got one in chemistry because she changed the theory immediately within a week of getting hard data that she trusted.

While the support of her colleagues may have bolstered Meitner's spirits, it did not change the reality: She had been passed over for the prize.

Oskar Klein, a member of the Royal Academy of Sciences, hoped that Meitner would be nominated and recognized in a subsequent year. Klein wrote to Niels Bohr:

> I regard it as a fairness, a needed rehabilitation after the underestimation—in any case on the part of the Swedish physicists—that she has had to put up with (and perhaps is still exposed to) and to which Hahn's references to her and Frisch's achievements undoubtedly contributed, while she has always been fair to Hahn in all her publications.

Bohr thought that Hahn's prize should not preclude Meitner and Frisch from winning in physics another year; he nominated them in 1946, 1947, and 1948, without success. In fact, Meitner was nominated for the Nobel Prize 15 times: 11 times for chemistry, nine of these with Otto Hahn and two with Otto Robert Frisch; and four times for physics, twice independently, once with Hahn, and once with Frisch. She never won the award.

Rewriting History

In the initial weeks and months after the atomic bomb was dropped, Meitner was often cited in newspaper and magazine articles explaining fission. In fact, Hahn was distressed to see Meitner's name in print so often with headlines such as "A Jewess Found the Clue" while his name was rarely mentioned at that time. Hahn wanted credit; he wanted to claim that fission was a German discovery—his discovery. Hahn now argued that Meitner had obstructed his research. His version of events failed to credit Meitner with her years of work done before being forced to leave Germany under dire circumstances. Instead of sharing the credit with Meitner, Hahn created his own version of events, that he and Strassmann "never touched upon physics, but only did chemical separations over and over again."

In 1939, Hahn may have distanced himself from Meitner and disavowed the work they had done together to protect himself from Nazi aggression, but in postwar 1945, he had every opportunity to set the record straight and acknowledge that he and Meitner had worked together—and that they both deserved credit for their contributions. Instead, Hahn stuck to his own version of history: That fission was a discovery of chemistry alone—his alone—in spite of years of work done by Meitner as a physicist.

Hahn told his story again and again until it had a life of its own. After he and the other German scientists were released from Farm Hall, those who had been detained with Hahn spread his version of events, effectively pushing Meitner out of the story of how fission was discovered. Rather than showing appreciation for Meitner's work, Hahn later called Meitner a bitter, disappointed woman who was jealous of his prize.

Making Sense of the War

In the postwar period, Meitner found Hahn's nationalism disturbing. When he returned home to Germany after being held in England, Hahn discovered food shortages, travel restrictions, and bombed-out public buildings. Hahn campaigned for postwar aid for Germany, noting how he and his countrymen were suffering. Meitner was concerned that Hahn seemed to have no remorse about Germany's actions during the war. She asked: "How can Germany regain the world's trust if the best Germans have already forgotten what happened?"

Meitner wanted her German friends to express their outrage over the gas chambers and other atrocities committed in their own country, to express both personal responsibility and collective, national guilt. For Meitner, looking the other way had been a crime; silence, a sin. She felt horror at not having left Germany earlier, at not having done something—anything—to attempt to stop the hideous crimes that had taken place right in front of her.

Hahn did not show regret; instead, he repeatedly stressed that Germany needed financial help in the postwar years. He argued that the Nazis had victimized Germany before and during the war and that the Allies were victimizing his country after the war. Meitner wondered: Did German citizens believe that they had any responsibility for their actions during the war?

Meitner was appalled that Hahn refused to apologize publicly for Germany's inhumane and barbaric behavior. She wrote:

> I do not think [the German people] comprehend just what
> fate has befallen Germany through their passivity. And
> they understand even less that they share responsibility for
> the horrible crimes Germany has committed. How shall
> the world trust a new Germany when its best and intel-
> lectually most prominent people do not have the insight to

understand this and do not have a burning desire to make whatever amends are possible?

In his discussions with Meitner, Hahn stressed that Germany had no responsibility for the atomic bomb, the most heinous weapon ever created. Meitner didn't debate the point, but she did remind Hahn that Germany had done many other terrible things and that one unspeakable horror does not diminish another. He did not respond.

Meitner argued that German scientists had offered too little, too late, in support of the Jews. She noted that the Academy of Science and the German Physical Society had expelled Einstein because he was Jewish. She cited the fact that scientific conferences had condemned "Jewish mathematics" and "Jewish physics." She saw Hahn as complicit in these acts against Jewish scientists because he had not taken a stand against them. Hahn "suppresses the past with all his might," she wrote. "Even though he always truly hated and despised the Nazis, since he does not have a very strong character and is not a very thoughtful person, he deceives himself."

The more Meitner learned about the German atrocities during the war, the more uncomfortable she became with Hahn's complacency. In 1945, she wrote to Hahn:

> When I heard a very objective report prepared by the British and Americans for the BBC about [the concentration camps] Bergen-Belsen and Buchenwald, I began to wail out loud and couldn't sleep all night. If only you had seen the people who came here from the camps. They should force a man like Heisenberg [a German physicist], and millions of others with him, to see these camps and the tortured people. . . . But you never had any sleepless nights: you didn't want to see—it was too disturbing. . . .

Hahn did not respond to her accusations.

The Nobel Ceremony

Meitner met Hahn and his wife Edith when they arrived in Stockholm a week before the Nobel Prize ceremony. Meitner went out of her way to take the Hahns sightseeing in Stockholm, shopping around the city, and dining with friends and colleagues. During interviews, she stood by and listened as Hahn made his plea for support for Germany and failed to mention anything about her.

The awards ceremony was held on December 10, 1946—the anniversary of the death of Alfred Nobel—in Stockholm, Sweden. Meitner attended as a guest. She wrote to a friend: "Like it or not, I must attend the Nobel banquet, which I've never done before. But if I don't go this time, when the Hahns are being honored, I fear it might be misunderstood."

At the time, the world was trying to make sense of the enormous destructive power demonstrated by the atomic bombings in Japan. When Hahn was introduced, the announcer said: "This discovery of fission of heavy nuclei has led to consequences of such a nature that all of us, indeed the whole of humanity, look forward with great expectations, but at the same time with great dread, to further developments."

In his remarks, Hahn acknowledged that the world had entered the nuclear age. He said: "The energy of nuclear physical reactions has been given into men's hands. Shall it be used for the assistance of free scientific thought, for social improvement and the betterment of the living conditions of mankind? Or will it be misused to destroy what mankind has built up in thousands of years?" Much of his lecture summarized the technical work that had been done on fission, but almost no mention was made of Meitner.

During and after the Nobel ceremonies Meitner was disappointed in Hahn both personally and politically. She was hurt and insulted that in Hahn's discussions with the press, he said as little as possible about their years of work together as research partners.

Worse yet, when he did mention her, he left reporters with the impression that Meitner had been a student or an assistant, but never an equal.

Meitner wrote to a friend: "I found it quite painful that in his interviews [Hahn] did not say one word about me, to say nothing of our 30 years together. His motivation is somewhat complicated. He is convinced that Germans are being treated unjustly, the more so in that he simply suppresses the past. Therefore while he was here his only thoughts were to speak for Germany. As for me, I am part of the suppressed past."

Moving On

In the postwar years, many scientists wanted to set the bomb aside and get back into the laboratory to develop peaceful uses for atomic power. In 1947, Hahn and Strassmann wrote to Meitner, offering back her old position at the Kaiser Wilhelm Institute, renamed the Max Planck Institutes for Chemistry after the war. Strassmann wrote that Hahn "was as convinced as I am that this would be the best solution for the Institute, but he did not think you would even consider such a proposal. Since I am an optimist, I will ask you anyway."

Hahn had been right: Meitner refused the offer.

She was not ready to return to Germany. Meitner wrote to a friend: "I personally believe that I cannot live in Germany. From all I see in letters from my German friends, and other things I hear about Germany, the Germans still do not comprehend what has happened, and they have completely forgotten all the horrors that did not personally happen to them. I think I would not be able to breathe in such an atmosphere." Meitner and Hahn did not work together again.

Although they had different views of the world, Meitner and Hahn remained bound to each other. Meitner didn't blame Hahn for his success in winning the Nobel Prize, but she did blame him for not crediting her contributions to his work. She didn't hold Hahn responsible for making regrettable compromises to survive in Hitler's Germany, but she did hold him responsible for not taking responsibility for the choices he made.

Ultimately, Meitner still loved Hahn like a brother with whom she disagreed on important issues, but a gap had grown between them. Meitner no longer trusted Hahn to be fair and supportive and to treat her as an equal. She was disappointed not only in what he said, but also what he failed to say. She continued to respect his intellect and his skill as a chemist, but through these experiences Meitner lost confidence in Hahn as a friend.

AFTERWORD:
PHYSICISTS, PACIFISTS, REALISTS

B Y THE END of World War II, science had transformed the world. Fission—the heart of this revolution—inspired leaders around the globe to reimagine what could be achieved by tapping into the power of the atom. The atomic bombs dropped on Japan demonstrated the monstrous power of fission in wartime; proposed plans to build nuclear power plants showed the potential of fission to provide an almost endless supply of energy in peacetime.

Harnessing the power of fission would not have happened without Irène Curie's discovery of artificial radioactivity and Lise Meitner's breakthrough in understanding the mechanism of dividing the atom. Both women saw science as a tool to improve society and enhance the lives of the next generation; both women were grief-stricken at the realization that fission was used to create the most powerful weapon of mass destruction that the world had ever known.

In the years after World War II, Meitner and the Joliot-Curies continued to work in their separate laboratories on the development of nuclear energy plants, but their postwar achievements were overshadowed by the important work they did in the years between World War I and World War II.

Irène

After the war, Irène served as a member of the French Atomic Energy Commission, and she became chair of the Department of Nuclear Physics and Radioactivity at the Sorbonne in Paris. She spent time attending and presenting at international conferences for peace, atomic weapon bans, and women's rights. Irène had accomplished more than almost any other scientist in France, but she did not meet her goal until 1949, when she achieved her ultimate ambition, the role she had been working toward for 30 years: She became director of the Curie Institute, just as her mother had been.

Even with her impressive credentials, Irène was denied membership in the French Academy of Sciences, the same group that had turned down her mother's application years before. Irène had tried to join and been refused several times, but she did not take the rejection personally. Rather than showing she was offended, Irène said, "Well, at least they are consistent in their thinking!"

Frédéric's career flourished in the first years after the war. French President Charles de Gaulle appointed him director of the National Center for Scientific Research, the most important research institute in France. When France created the world's first civilian Atomic Energy Commission, de Gaulle appointed Frédéric director of that as well. As head of the Atomic Energy Commission, Frédéric oversaw France's first nuclear reactor as it began operations on December 15, 1948.

Frédéric and Irène's popularity did not last. The Joliot-Curies had trouble during the violently anticommunist 1950s because of their politics: Frédéric was an acknowledged member of the Communist Party, and Irène was an antifascist, married to a communist.

The United States government kept an eye on Irène when she traveled to New York City in 1948 to speak at several fundraisers benefitting refugees of the Spanish Civil War. When Irène and her mother toured the United States in 1921, they were celebrated as national

Irène Joliot-Curie was active with the Joint Anti-Fascist Refugee Committee and spoke at various fundraisers in support of the group.

heroes; this time the U.S. immigration authorities initially would not even allow Irène to enter the country and detained her overnight in a cell on Ellis Island. The United States attorney general considered the group sponsoring her trip, the Joint Anti-Fascist Refugee Committee, subversive. The House Un-American Activities Committee had recently investigated her host, Dr. Edward Barsky, a New York surgeon, about his work with the refugee Committee. He had refused to turn over his records, so he was found in contempt of court and sentenced to six months in jail. Because Barsky had been involved with this suspect activity, Irène was considered guilty by association.

The following day, French authorities protested Irène's detention, and she was released. Reporters interviewed her and asked about her night in jail: Irène said that Ellis Island's accommodations were adequate and that she had enjoyed some good coffee and a chance to darn her stockings. She also explained that she was not and never had been a communist, adding: "I am not surprised to have been arrested and detained, because I am here to aid the anti-fascists. And, in the United States, they prefer the fascists and even the Nazis to the communists. They think that the first and second [the fascists and Nazis] have more respect for money."

Despite the bumpy beginning, the rest of Irène's tour in the United States went without disruption. When she wrote to Frédéric, she reported that once she got out of New York City the press was fair and friendly, and 900 people attended a banquet held in her honor before she left.

At the same time, Frédéric's politics began to get him in trouble in France. Frédéric insisted that fission should be used only for peaceful purposes, while the French and United States governments were planning to build a hydrogen bomb. As the Cold War and McCarthyism intensified in the United States, the American government pressured the French to fire Frédéric. In 1950, he was let go from his post at the French Atomic Energy Commission. The following year, Irène's term expired and she was not asked to remain on the Commission because she refused to denounce the Communist Party.

At that point, both Irène and Frédéric were further marginalized due to their politics. In 1951, Irène traveled to Stockholm to attend a physics conference, and hotels in the city refused to give her a room. Later, the British government denied her a visa to attend another scientific conference. Despite the fact that she had won the Nobel Prize, the American Chemical Society rejected her application for membership. Even former friends spent less time with the Joliot-Curies because they worried that their reputations might be compromised by association.

Undaunted, Irène continued to work on scientific problems that interested her. In 1955 she designed a new nuclear physics center and particle accelerator, which eventually would be constructed at the University of Orsay (France) in 1958. She also had more time to spend with her family, including her daughter, Hélène, who had become a nuclear physicist, and her son, Pierre, who had become a biophysicist specializing in photosynthesis.

"I am not afraid of death"

Irène had suffered from tuberculosis for years, often spending weeks or months at a time recovering in a sanatorium. Her condition finally improved after the war when Marie Curie's friend Missy Meloney sent Irène a new antibiotic, streptomycin, which cured the disease. (The drug, the first known to cure tuberculosis, was developed and tested in the United States in 1946.) Throughout the late 1940s and early 1950s, Irène's health was better than it had been in decades, although years of exposure to radiation had already caused irreparable long-term damage.

Irène worked in the lab every day through January 1956. In February of that year, she went alone to the family's ski chalet in the Alps for a brief retreat. Once she arrived, she felt seriously ill, so she took a train back to Paris and checked herself into the hospital. She never checked out.

A lifetime of handling radioactive elements had caught up with her: Doctors diagnosed leukemia, the same illness that had taken her mother's life. At the time, Frédéric was so sick with radiation-induced hepatitis that he could manage to see Irène for only a few minutes at a time. Her condition was dire; Irène knew that she was going to die. She told a childhood friend: "I am not afraid of death. I have had such a thrilling life!"

Irène Joliot-Curie died of leukemia at the age of 58 on March 17, 1956.

Ironically, the same radioactivity that caused Irène's leukemia later became a treatment for the disease. To cure some forms of leukemia, doctors now inject their patients with controlled doses of radioactive isotopes—isotopes that would not have been developed without the Joliot-Curies' discovery of artificial radioactivity. This

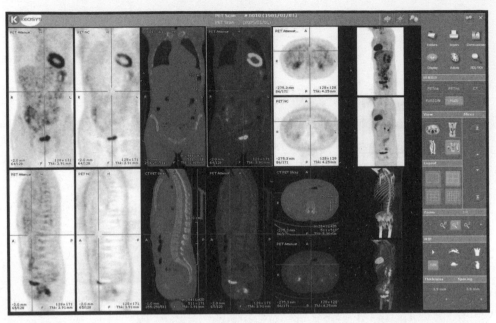

Scientists have created hundreds of different radioactive isotopes, which can be used to produce three-dimensional images of metabolic processes in the body, as shown here. Nuclear medicine is often used to identify cancerous tumors in the body.

remedy may have come too late for Irène, but her work provided the foundation for medical research that has saved countless lives.

Frédéric had been certain that he would die before Irène, so he was unprepared to handle the emotional loss when she died. He wrote to Otto Hahn in response to a letter of condolence: "I have had some very hard moments but I have been able to find the strength necessary to resist by working like fury."

Two years later, Frédéric died, also of leukemia, which he called "our occupational disease."

Lise

Although she did not win the Nobel Prize, in October 1945 Lise Meitner learned that she had been elected a Foreign Member of the Swedish Royal Academy of Sciences. In its 200 years of existence, the Academy had bestowed the honor on only two other women: Eva Ekeblad in 1748 and Marie Curie in 1910.

That same fall, Meitner accepted an invitation to teach for a semester at Catholic University in Washington, D.C., and to lecture at a number of other universities, including Harvard, Princeton, and the Massachusetts Institute of Technology. In addition to the excitement of meeting other experts in her field, Meitner also looked forward to having the chance to spend time with two of her sisters, who had moved to the United States.

When she arrived in New York in January 1946, Meitner discovered that she was considered a celebrity. Although she had been denied the Nobel Prize, in the early postwar years she received widespread recognition for her work on fission. The Women's National Press Club chose her as their 1946 Woman of the Year, and she had the honor of sitting next to President Harry Truman at the awards dinner. When he met Meitner, President Truman, referring to the creation of the atomic bomb, said: "So you're the little lady who got us into all of this!" Of course, Meitner had never worked on weapons research, and she supported the international peace movement. She did not want to be associated with the atomic bomb; her interest in science had only been academic, not militaristic.

Lise Meitner lecturing at Catholic University in Washington, D.C., 1946.

During her six-month stay in the United States, Meitner was interviewed by a number of reporters and journalists, including a writer for the *Saturday Evening Post* in 1946. In the *Post* article she said:

> . . . I do not see why everybody is making such a fuss over
> me. I did not design any atomic bomb. I don't even know
> what one looks like, nor how it works technically. The great
> strides of atomic science are the results of the combined ef-
> forts of all atom[ic] workers. We strove toward a common
> goal, pooling our knowledge. I must stress that I myself have
> not in any way worked on the smashing of the atom with
> the idea of producing death-dealing weapons. You must
> not blame us scientists for the use to which war technicians
> have put our discoveries. . . . We must not be led into draw-
> ing too-pessimistic conclusions just because the first use to
> which atomic energy was put happened to be in an engine of
> destruction. We must look at it as a revolutionizing scientific
> discovery; but perhaps, even so, only the first step on the
> road to something greater and still more valuable—
> mastering the art of using atomic energy for the benefit of
> mankind.

After leaving the United States, Meitner decided to return to
Sweden. In 1947, a position was created for her at Sweden's Royal
Institute of Technology, with funding from the Council for Atomic
Research. At last, Meitner had a laboratory of her own, with equipment and assistants and a reliable salary. She was able to do her own
research there, including work on Sweden's first nuclear power plant,
which became operational in 1954. She became a Swedish citizen in
1949, and worked until she retired in 1953 at age 75. Even after retirement, Meitner continued to attend lectures and seminars, super-
vise graduate students, and work closely with doctoral candidates.

After the war, Hahn became a celebrated scientist in Germany.
He was one of the few German scientists trusted by the Allies, and
he became president of the Max Planck Society. Germans recognized

him as an iconic scientific figure; his image appeared on German medals, buildings, coins, and stamps.

Otto Hahn was not Meitner's only German colleague eager to erase his Nazi-era history. In 1947, Meitner received letters from several former colleagues who had been Nazi Party members and now wanted her to act as references during "denazification," a program to remove Nazi Party members from positions of influence in postwar Germany. One request came from a colleague who said that his Nazi Party membership had been a mistake; he begged her to write a letter on his behalf saying that he had been an ineffective Nazi. "You would be one of the best to give an opinion of me," he wrote. She received a similar letter from a former assistant, who had brought charges against her in 1934. He had three children and he was threatened with losing his job and possible arrest. He told her that he regretted what he had done to her and promised that his behavior had been "not political or anti-Semitic . . . but based on an immature character . . . [that] could, as a man, subordinate itself professionally to a woman only with inner resistance. Very respected Frau Professor Meitner, if you can answer me in my need quite soon, I would be exceptionally grateful."

In an act of astonishing compassion, Meitner wrote letters on behalf of both men. She considered the process of denazification to be ridiculous and meaningless, since those involved would simply make false statements to protect themselves. Choosing her words carefully, she wrote for the first man: "I knew very little about the details of your [political] membership and position, so in that sense I can state . . . that you did not propagate Nazi ideas or express them by your manner." For the other colleague she wrote: "The motives of personal relationships, good and bad, are usually much more complicated than they may seem. . . . I am certainly willing to believe that anti-Semitism was not the driving force for you."

A prosecutor contacted Meitner about Kurt Hess, the strident Nazi from the Kaiser Wilhelm Institute who reviled her and tried to have her arrested before she had a chance to flee Germany in 1938. In an attempt to assess Hess's culpability, the prosecutor in his case sent Meitner a list of detailed questions about his behavior. In that moment, she had the power to indict or exonerate him. She chose to remain silent; she threw the letter away and did not respond.

Meitner's ability to forgive made it possible for her to remain friends with Hahn. Over the years their relationship had changed many times. As they grew older, Meitner began to act a bit like an older sister, teasing him and calling him "Hahnchen" (the diminutive of "Hahn"). Whenever he said anything about physics, she would chastise him: "Be quiet, Hahnchen, you don't understand physics." When they were almost 80 years old, Meitner and Hahn were walking up steps at an awards ceremony and she whispered: "Keep your back straight, Otto. Otherwise they'll think we're old."

Meitner lived in Sweden for 22 years, visiting the United States several times to work and see relatives. In 1953, when she was 75 years old, she fell down a flight of stairs at a physics conference, but she pulled herself up, uninjured, and resumed her conversation. She continued with her research and climbed mountains for exercise until she was 81 years old.

In 1960, Meitner moved to Cambridge, England, to be near her nephew, Otto Frisch, who had become chairman of the natural philosophy department at Cambridge University. She continued to travel and lecture, but not as much as she once had. During a trip to the United States in 1964 Meitner suffered a heart attack, and it took her several months to recover.

In 1966, the United States Atomic Energy Commission presented the Enrico Fermi Award to the entire fission team: Meitner, Hahn, and Strassmann. It may not have been the Nobel Prize, but the prestigious Fermi Award was evidence that the international scientific community finally recognized Meitner's work on fission. It was the first time that non-Americans had received the prize and the first time that a woman had won it. Meitner was too frail to go to

Lise Meitner and Otto Hahn chatted together in West Germany in 1962.

Vienna to accept the award, so it was presented to her at her home. She used the $15,000 she received in prize money to establish a library at Cambridge University for her papers.

After breaking her hip in a fall and suffering several small strokes in 1967, Meitner moved into a nursing home in Cambridge, England. She died on October 27, 1968, at the age of 89. She was buried in the village of Bramley in Hampshire, England, close to her beloved brother, Walter. Frisch had her headstone inscribed: "Lise Meitner: A physicist who never lost her humanity."

Fifteen years after Meitner's death, physicists in Darmstadt, Germany, fused together isotopes of bismuth and iron to make Element 109, which was the heaviest known element in the universe at the time. It took another fifteen years for the researchers to gain approval for their chosen name, but in 1997 the physicists who synthesized this new element named it meitnerium, in honor of Lise Meitner.

IN THE YEARS SINCE their deaths, the names Irène Curie and
Lise Meitner have been largely forgotten. While the Curie name
may have opened doors and provided opportunities for Irène during
her lifetime, her mother's achievements and acclaim ultimately overshadowed Irène's accomplishments. Mention the name "Curie" and
most people think of Marie, not Irène. Both women were brilliant
scientists who deserve to be recognized and remembered in their
own right.

Meitner's reputation was undermined by Otto Hahn's systematic
attempts to take credit for the discovery of fission, credit that they
should have shared. Meitner and Hahn worked together for more
than 30 years and they coauthored more than 50 articles published
in scientific journals, but when it came to the crowning achievement of their careers—the discovery of fission—Meitner was denied
status as a member of the team. Hahn chose to perpetuate the myth
that he had discovered fission alone, despite the evidence that he
had depended on Meitner to interpret and explain the results of his
research. The fact that she had to flee Germany during Hitler's reign
of terror meant that Meitner could not be present to defend her
place in history.

While these two often overlooked women of science may not
have the name recognition of other first-rate physicists of the 20th
century, their contributions are undeniable. Without Irène Curie's
discovery of artificial radioactivity and Lise Meitner's breakthrough
in the understanding of fission, the atomic age—which has produced nuclear energy and nuclear medicine, as well as the deadly
weapon that changed the course of human history—would not have
been possible.

TIME LINE

	1878	Lise Meitner is born, Vienna, Austria, on November 7
Irène Curie is born, Paris, France, on September 12	**1897**	
	1901	Meitner admitted to the University of Vienna
Marie and Pierre Curie and Antoine Henri Becquerel win the Nobel Prize in Physics	**1903**	
	1905	Meitner graduates from University of Vienna with a doctorate in physics
	1907	Meitner moves to Berlin; works at the University of Berlin; partners with Otto Hahn
Marie Curie wins the Nobel Prize in Chemistry	**1911**	
	1912	Meitner moves to the Kaiser Wilhelm Institute (KWI) in Dahlem, Germany
	1914	
	WORLD WAR I BEGINS IN EUROPE	
	1917	Meitner discovers the element protactinium with Otto Hahn
	1918	
	END OF WORLD WAR I	

	1923	Meitner becomes a lecturer at the University of Berlin Physics Department
Irène earns Doctorate of Science	**1925**	
Irène marries Frédéric Joliot	**1926**	
Hélène Langevin-Joliot born	**1927**	
Pierre Joliot born	**1932**	
Irène and Frédéric Joliot-Curie win Nobel Prize in Chemistry	**1935**	
	1938	Meitner flees Germany; goes to Netherlands
	1938	Meitner discovers fission
	1939	Meitner publishes article describing nuclear fission with nephew Otto Frisch

1939
WORLD WAR II BEGINS IN EUROPE

Curium, element 96, is named for Marie and Pierre. (The discovery was not made public until 1945.)	**1944**	
	1944	Meitner overlooked as Otto Hahn is awarded Nobel Prize in Chemistry for the discovery of nuclear fission

1945
ATOMIC BOMBS DROPPED ON JAPAN
END OF WORLD WAR II

	1945	Meitner elected a foreign member of the Royal Swedish Academy of Sciences
Irène becomes Director of the Radium Institute	**1946**	
	1946	Meitner awarded Woman of the Year by the National Press Club in the United States
	1949	Meitner awarded Max Planck Medal with Otto Hahn
Irène Curie dies on March 17 at age 58	**1956**	
	1960	Meitner elected a foreign member of the American Academy of Sciences
	1966	Meitner wins the Enrico Fermi Award with Otto Hahn and Fritz Strassmann
	1968	Lise Meitner dies on October 27 at age 89
	1997	Meitnerium, element 109, is named in Lise Meitner's honor

GLOSSARY

....

Alpha particles are made of two protons and two neutrons bound together; they are identical in structure to a helium nucleus and are produced during alpha decay. Alpha decay is the process in which an alpha particle is ejected from the nucleus of a radioactive atom.

Atoms are the basic units of matter. They are made of a dense nucleus surrounded by negatively charged electrons circulating in areas known as electron clouds. The nucleus is made up of positively charged protons and electrically neutral neutrons.

Atomic number refers to the number of protons in the nucleus of an atom. This determines an element's place on the periodic table, as well as its chemical properties, such as melting point, boiling point, and how it reacts with other elements. In an uncharged or neutral atom, the atomic number is also equal to the number of electrons.

Beta particles are electrons or positrons ejected from the nucleus of radioactive atoms. Beta decay is the process in which a beta particle (an electron or positron) is ejected from the nucleus of a radioactive atom.

Chain reaction is a sequence of events in which the product of one reaction triggers the next reaction.

A decay series, also known as a **decay chain** or **decay sequence**, is a series of decay processes or transformations in which one element decays to create a new element that may or may not be radioactive. The chain ends when a stable element or isotope is formed. For example, uranium-238 decays to form radium-226, which decays to form radon-222, which decays to form polonium-210, which decays to form lead-206, which is the final, stable element at the end of the chain.

Electrons are subatomic particles with a negative charge. They orbit the nucleus of an atom inside an electron cloud.

Fission or **nuclear fission** is a reaction in which an atom's nucleus breaks into smaller parts. Fission typically gives off neutrons and photons, as well as a great deal of energy. Fission is a form of **transmutation** because the resulting fragments aren't the same elements or the original atom.

Gamma rays are a type of electromagnetic radiation with extremely high energy. They naturally occur during the decay of radioactive isotopes. They can also come from lightning strikes or various astronomical processes, as well as nuclear fission during a nuclear explosion. Gamma rays can harm human tissue and cause cancer.

Half-life refers to the amount of time required for half of the unstable radioactive atoms in a sample to decay. For example, the half-life of carbon-14 is 5,730 years. That means that half of a sample will have decayed in 5,730 years, and half of that amount will decay after another 5,730 years (leaving one-quarter of the original amount). In other words, three-fourths of the original sample will have decayed after 11,460 years.

Heavy water, also known as deuterium oxide or D_2O, is an atom of water that consists of a hydrogen isotope with an extra neutron. The hydrogen atoms in heavy water contain a neutron, making them about twice as heavy as typical hydrogen atoms. Ordinary water has about 156 molecules of deuterium per million; heavy water has 997,500 molecules of deuterium per million. This makes heavy water about 11 percent denser than ordinary water.

Ions are atoms with a positive or negative electrical charge created by an uneven number of electrons and protons.

Isotopes are variations of an element. While isotopes of an element have the same number of protons, they have different numbers of neutrons. For example, carbon-12, carbon-13, and carbon-14 are all isotopes of carbon. Since all carbon atoms have 6 protons, these isotopes have 6, 7, or 8 neutrons, respectively. Different isotopes of a single element occupy the same spot on the periodic table. Isotopes are different from **ions**, which are atoms with a different number of electrons than protons.

Neutrons are subatomic particles with no electric charge. They have a mass that is nearly equal to that of a proton. They are found in the nucleus of atoms.

Nuclear reactors are devices used to create a sustained nuclear chain reaction using fission. Typically they are used at nuclear power plants and to power nuclear submarines and ships. To control the rate of reaction, nuclear reactors rely on heavy water, ordinary water, or solid graphite.

The **periodic table** is a chart listing the chemical elements based on their atomic number, chemical properties, and electron configurations. The standard format consists of 18 columns and seven rows, with two additional rows beneath that. The table design shows repeating patterns that can be used to establish relationships between the elements.

Positrons, also known as **antielectrons**, are the antimatter or antiparticle counterparts to electrons (that is, they have the same mass but the opposite electric charge). Positrons are generated by radioactive decay or by photons.

Protons are subatomic particles with a positive electric charge that cancels out the negative electron charge. One or more protons exist in the nucleus of each atom. The number of protons in the nucleus determines the atomic number. Each element has a different atomic number.

Subatomic particles are the components of an atom, including protons, neutrons, and electrons.

Transmutation, or **nuclear transmutation**, is the change of one element or isotope to another as a result of a nuclear reaction.

Transuranic elements, also known as **transuranium elements**, are elements with atomic numbers greater than 92. They are created in a lab rather than found in nature. All of the transuranic elements are unstable and undergo radioactive decay to form other, more stable, elements.

Uranium is a metallic element with the atomic number 92. The most common isotopes of uranium are U-238, which has 146 neutrons and accounts for 99.3 percent of the uranium found in nature, and U-235, which has 143 neutrons and accounts for 0.7 percent of the uranium in nature. U-235 is less stable and can therefore be used in a sustained nuclear reaction.

WHO'S WHO

....

Carl David Anderson (1905–1991): American physicist who discovered the positron in 1932. He won the Nobel Prize in Physics in 1936.

Antoine Henri Becquerel (1852–1908): French physicist who discovered natural radioactivity. He shared the Nobel Prize in Physics with Marie and Pierre Curie in 1903. He was also an expert in solar radiation and phosphorescence.

Niels Bohr (1885–1962): Danish physicist who studied quantum theory and atomic structure; he designed the Bohr model of the atom. He won the Nobel Prize in Physics in 1922.

Ludwig Boltzmann (1844–1906): Austrian physicist who developed statistical mechanics, which predicts how properties of matter affect their physical properties. He inspired Lise Meitner when she was a student at the University of Vienna. He suffered from bipolar disorder and hanged himself at age 62.

James Chadwick (1891–1974): English physicist who discovered the neutron in 1932. He won the Nobel Prize in Physics in 1935.

Dirk Coster (1889–1950): Dutch physicist and professor at University of Groningen. He helped to arrange Lise Meitner's escape from Germany in July 1938.

Albert Einstein (1879–1955): German theoretical physicist who developed the general theory of relativity. His mass-energy equivalence formula, $E=mc^2$, inspired Meitner in her discovery of fission. He won the Nobel Prize in Physics in 1921.

Enrico Fermi (1901–1954): Italian physicist known for his work on the first nuclear reactor, Chicago Pile-1. He is often called the "father of the atomic bomb." He won the Nobel Prize in Physics in 1938.

Hermann Emil Fischer (1852–1919): German chemist who did ground-breaking work on sugars. He won the Nobel Prize in Chemistry in 1902. He operated the laboratory first shared by Lise Meitner and Otto Hahn.

Adriaan Fokker (1887–1972): Dutch physicist and musician. He helped Lise Meitner escape from Germany in July 1938.

James Franck (1882–1964): German experimental physicist who confirmed the Bohr model of the atom. He won the Nobel Prize in Physics in 1925. As a Jew, he was forced to resign his post at the University of Berlin when Hitler came to power in 1933. He worked with the Manhattan Project, although he objected to the use of the atomic bomb.

Otto Robert Frisch (1904–1979): Austrian-British physicist who coined the term "fission" in his discussion with his aunt, Lise Meitner. He designed the first theoretical mechanism for the detonation of an atomic bomb in 1940.

Otto Hahn (1879–1968): German chemist and Lise Meitner's research partner for more than 30 years. He is called "the father of nuclear chemistry." He won the Nobel Prize in Chemistry in 1944. He was president of the Kaiser Wilhelm Society in 1946 and founding president of the Max Planck Society from 1948 to 1960.

Adolf Hitler (1889–1945): Austrian-born German politician. He was chancellor of Germany from 1933 to 1945 and dictator of Nazi Germany from 1934 to 1945.

Pierre Joliot-Curie (1932–): French biologist and researcher at the French National Center for Scientific Research. He is the son of Irène and Frédéric Joliot-Curie and a member of the Academy of Science of France.

Eve Curie Labouisse (1904–2007): Youngest daughter of Marie and Pierre Curie. She was a writer, journalist, and pianist. She wrote her mother's biography, *Madame Curie*, in 1937.

Paul Langevin (1872–1946): French physicist who created an underwater submarine detector and was a close friend of Marie and Pierre Curie. He was president of the Human Rights League from 1944 to 1946. He had a well-publicized affair with Marie in 1911. His grandson and Marie's granddaughter (Irène and Frédéric Joliot-Curie's daughter) married.

Hélène Langevin-Joliot (1927–): French nuclear physicist and daughter of Irène and Frédéric Joliot-Curie. She was a professor of nuclear physics at the Institute of Nuclear Physics at the University of Paris. Hélène married Michel Langevin, the grandson of Paul Langevin; the two met while studying physics and chemistry. Her father asked her to use the name Langevin-Joliot, rather than simply Langevin.

Marie "Missy" Mattingly Meloney (1878–1943): American journalist, magazine editor, and socialite. She orchestrated the fund drive for radium for Marie Curie, and arranged Curie's visit to the United States in 1921.

Alfred Nobel (1833–1896): Swedish chemist, engineer, and inventor. He held more than 350 different patents, including one for dynamite. He used his fortune to fund the Nobel Prizes.

Ida Noddak (1896–1978): German chemist and physicist who first mentioned the possibility of fission in an article in 1934. The article was dismissed because she did not offer any supporting evidence for the theory she proposed.

Wolfgang Pauli (1900–1958): Austrian-Swiss theoretical physicist and a pioneer of quantum physics. He won the Nobel Prize in Physics in 1945.

Max Planck (1858–1947): German theoretical physicist who originated quantum theory and won the Nobel Prize in Physics in 1918.

Wilhelm Röntgen (1845–1923): German physicist who discovered X-rays, also called Röntgen rays, in 1895 and winner of the first Nobel Prize in Physics in 1901.

Ernest Rutherford (1871–1937): New Zealand-born British physicist known as the "father of nuclear physics." He developed the concept of radioactive half-life, recognized the distinction between alpha and beta radiation, and he developed the Rutherford model of the atom. He won the Nobel Prize in Chemistry in 1908.

Karl Manne Siegbahn (1886–1978): Swedish physicist known for his work on X-ray spectroscopy, which is used to identify elements based on the X-ray wavelengths they produce. He won the Nobel Prize in Physics in 1924.

Friedrich Wilhelm "Fritz" Strassmann (1902–1980): German chemist who worked with Otto Hahn in the experiments that resulted in the discovery of nuclear fission. He refused to cooperate with the Nazi Party and was blacklisted as a result.

Leó Szilárd (1898–1964): Hungarian physicist and inventor. He conceived of a nuclear chain reaction in 1933, and he and Enrico Fermi patented the idea of the nuclear reactor. In 1939 he and Albert Einstein wrote a letter to President Franklin D. Roosevelt, which resulted in the Manhattan Project.

Charles Wilson (1869–1959): Scottish physicist and meteorologist who created the Wilson cloud chamber, a device that used cloud trails to show the movement of subatomic particles. He won the Nobel Prize in Physics in 1927.

CHAPTER NOTES

....

Chapter 1: "The Most Beautiful Experiment in the World"

"Physics is once again very fouled up . . ." McGrayne, Sharon Bertsch. *Nobel Prize Women in Science: Their Lives, Struggles and Momentous Discoveries*. Washington, D.C.: Joseph Henry Press, 1993; p. 117.

"My colleagues and I have done similar experiments . . ." Pflaum, Rosalynd. *Grand Obsession: Madame Curie and Her World*. New York: Doubleday, 1989; p. 302.

"What you are doing is of the greatest importance," Pflaum, Rosalynd. *Marie Curie and Her Daughter Irène*. Minneapolis: Lerner Publications, 1993; p. 121.

"Congratulations, don't give up," Pflaum, Rosalynd. *Grand Obsession,* p. 303.

"An infinitely tiny particle projected . . ." Quinn, Susan. *Marie Curie: A Life*. New York: Da Capo Press, 1996; p. 428.

"Scientists, building up or shattering elements . . ." Quinn, p. 429.

"I will never forget the expression of intense joy . . ." Dry, Sarah. *Curie*. London: Haus Publishing, 2003; p. 124.

"The significance of these extraordinarily beautiful results . . ." Sime, Ruth Lewin. *Lise Meitner: A Life in Physics*. Berkeley, California: University of California Press, 1996; p. 162.

"The question was entirely new . . ." Redniss, Lauren. *Radioactive: Marie & Pierre Curie: A Tale of Love and Fallout*. New York: It Books, 2011; p. 42.

Chapter 2: Little Queen and the Other Baby

"Little Queen . . ." McGrayne, p. 118.

"*Mé! Mé!*" Pflaum, *Marie Curie and Her Daughter Irène*, p. 54.

"These gleamings . . ." Redniss, p. 60.

"The child to whom she had given . . ." Des Jardins, Julie. *The Madame Curie Complex: The Hidden History of Women in Science.* New York: The Feminist Press at CUNY, 2010; p. 32.

"My spirit had been formed . . ." McGrayne, p. 121.

"You must take notice . . ." McGrayne, p. 122.

"At the laboratory . . ." McGrayne, p. 122.

"On the 42nd day . . ." Redniss, p. 70.

"Resembled her father . . ." McGrayne, p. 122.

"When I have a book . . ." McGrayne, p. 124.

"It is not necessary to mix . . ." Pflaum, *Marie Curie and Her Daughter Irène*, pp. 53–54.

"He used to say . . ." Des Jardins, p. 32.

"One can imagine . . ." Pflaum, *Grand Obsession*, p. 124–25.

"She is too young . . ." Pflaum, *Grand Obsession*, p. 132.

"I couldn't bear to have anyone . . ." Pflaum, *Grand Obsession*, p. 135.

"WHEN ARE YOU COMING . . ." Pflaum, *Marie Curie and Her Daughter Irène*, p. 69.

"I love you very much . . ." McGrayne, p. 124.

"Go home . . ." Emling, Shelley. *Marie Curie and her Daughters: The Private Lives of Science's First Family.* New York: Palgrave Macmillan, 2012; p. 8.

Chapter 3: On the Battlefields

"If I am there . . ." Curie, Eve. *Madame Curie: A Biography.* New York: Doubleday, 1937; reprint, DaCapo Press, 2001; p. 292.

"[We] are beginning to face . . ." Curie, p. 292.

"Things are not going very well . . ." Curie, p. 292.

"My sweet dear . . ." McGrayne, p. 126.

"I was rather amused . . ." Quinn, p. 369.

"Surmounted the little difficulties . . ." McGrayne, p. 118.

"I spent my birthday admirably . . ." Quinn, p. 370.

Chapter 4: Dr. and Mrs.

"Crown Princess of Science," Pflaum, *Marie Curie and Her Daughter Irène*, p. 100.

"Irène not only called a spade a spade . . ." McGrayne, p. 127.

"I never heard her say . . ." McGrayne, p. 127.

"I was very different from her . . ." McGrayne, p. 126.

"You know, my child, that you are . . ." McGrayne, p. 127.

"She will see no one . . ." Des Jardins, p. 23.

"The Greatest Woman in the World," Pflaum, *Marie Curie and Her Daughter Irène*, p. 92.

"Miss Radium Eyes," McGrayne, p. 127.

"Peasant-like," Pflaum, *Marie Curie and Her Daughter Irène*, p. 93.

"To Madame Curie . . ." McGrayne, p. 128.

"Not at all . . ." McGrayne, p. 128.

"Opposites at *everything* . . ." McGrayne, p. 129.

"I discovered in this girl . . ." McGrayne, p. 129.

"When I married . . ." McGrayne, p. 130.

"I miss Irène a lot . . ." Quinn, p. 426.

"The man who married . . ." McGrayne, p. 130.

"My mother and my husband . . ." McGrayne, p. 130.

"The boy is a skyrocket," McGrayne, p. 130.

"The Prince Consort . . ." McGrayne, p. 130.

"Why are people so nasty?" McGrayne, p. 131.

"Funny, you have a bee in your bonnet . . ." Pflaum, *Grand Obsession*, p. 279.

"M. Frédéric Joliot-Curie is certainly a great man . . ." Pflaum, *Grand Obsession*, p. 279.

Chapter 5: Right on Time

"The Emission of Protons . . ." Pflaum, *Marie Curie and Her Daughter Irène*, p. 115.

"I don't believe it . . ." McGrayne, p. 133.

"A few days of strenuous work . . ." Quinn, p. 427.

"It is annoying to be overtaken . . ." Preston, Diana. *Before the Fallout: From Marie Curie to Hiroshima*. New York: Berkley Books, 2005; p. 74.

"Immediately, clearly, and convincingly," Preston, p. 74.

"Going backwards the wrong way," Preston, p. 91.

"With the neutron we were too late . . ." Emling, p. 131.

"I am the only one of the family . . ." Emling, p. 207.

"In our family, we are accustomed . . ." McGrayne, p. 136.

"Fame was something from the outside . . ." Pflaum, *Marie Curie and Her Daughter Irène*, p. 106.

Chapter 6: Lost and Found

"Listen to me . . ." Rife, Patricia. *Lise Meitner and the Dawn of the Nuclear Age*. Boston: Birkhausen, 1999; p. 2.

"That there were such things . . ." Rife, p. 3.

"Life need not be easy . . ." McGrayne, p. 38.

"Lost years," McGrayne, p. 38.

"Nothing else has to be done . . ." McGrayne, p. 38.

"Lise, you're going to flunk . . ." McGrayne, p. 41.

"Musical heaven," McGrayne, p. 41.

"When I registered with Planck . . ." Rife, pp. 20–21.

"If a woman has a special gift . . ." Rife, p. 21.

"A rare honesty of mind . . ." McGrayne, p. 43.

"Hahn was of the same age..." Rife, p. 26.

"When I think back . . ." Rife, pp. 31–32.

"Oh, I thought you were a man!" McGrayne, p. 45.

"He was much better known . . ." McGrayne, p. 45.

"Oh, my dear, I just didn't have . . ." McGrayne, p. 45.

"There was no question . . ." McGrayne, p. 45.

Chapter 7: A Lab of Her Own

"They were also exceptionally nice . . ." McGrayne, p. 47.

"Radioactivity and atomic physics . . ." Rife, p. 38.

"That colloquium was the greatest event . . ." McGrayne, p. 50.

"By 1907 these colloquia were already . . ." Rife, p. 37.

"A magic, musical accompaniment . . ." McGrayne, p. 50.

"At that time I did not yet realize . . ." Rife, p. 44.

"Guest," Rife, p. 50.

"Not only did this give me a chance . . ." Rife, p. 46.

"We are converting . . ." Sime, p. 60.

"You can hardly imagine . . ." Rife, p. 62.

"First, we attacked . . ." Rife, p. 70.

"As a result of continuous work . . ." Sime, p. 58.

"It was a way of saving countless lives . . ." Preston, p. 53.

"Our German Madame Curie," Rife, p. 86.

"Loosening the energy of the atom . . ." Rife, p. 104.

"Anyone who expects a source of power . . ." Rife, p. 104.

"I love physics with all my heart . . ." Rife, p. 56.

Chapter 8: Radium: Treatment or Toxin?

"In very bad health . . ." Dry, p. 115.

"Unjustified fears," Quinn, p. 412.

"Industrial establishments which prepare . . ." Quinn, p. 413.

"Irène doesn't feel well . . ." Quinn, p. 415.

Chapter 9: Heavy Metals

"For Hahn it was like the old days . . ." McGrayne, pp. 52–53.

"The first thing Hahn and Meitner did . . ." Rife, p. 143.

"We regret this very much . . ." Rife, p. 153.

"Still relying on the chemical knowledge . . ." Preston, p. 104.

"Curiousium," Sime, p. 183.

"Committed gross error . . ." Rife, p. 155.

"Lost interest in the situation . . ." Sime, p. 183.

"Between us, my dear . . ." McGrayne, p. 139.

"Cannot be anything except a transuranic element . . ." Sime, p. 183.

Chapter 10: Fleeing Hitler's Germany

"According to the law of April 1, 1933 . . ." Rife, p. 114.

"Planck once said . . ." Rife, pp. 114–15.

"Hitler answered me literally . . ." Rife, p. 137.

"Immediately! For the reason set forth . . ." Rife, p. 124.

"Too valuable to annoy," McGrayne, p. 54.

"A very strong feeling of solidarity . . ." McGrayne, p. 54.

"As long as it's only us . . ." McGrayne, p. 54.

"The years of the Hitler regime . . ." Rhodes, Richard. *The Making of the Atomic Bomb: The 25th Anniversary Edition*. New York: Simon & Schuster, 2012; p. 235.

"The Jewess endangers this Insistute . . ." McGrayne, p. 54.

"I rather lost my nerve . . ." Rife, p. 163.

"I always remember that Lise . . ." McGrayne, p. 54.

"It is considered undesirable . . ." Rife, p. 166.

"The local Physical Society and the Chemistry Association . . ." Sime, p. 187.

"Offer a one-year appointment," Rife, p. 169.

"The assistant we talked about . . ." Rife, p. 171.

"SAT 9 JULY/I AM COMING . . ." Rife, p. 171.

"Friendly persuasion," Rife, p. 173.

"For urgent emergencies," Rife, p. 172.

"I took a train for Holland . . ." Rhodes, p. 236.

"I want to congratulate you . . ." Hamilton, Janet. *Lise Meitner: Pioneer of Nuclear Fission.* Berkeley Heights, NJ: Enslow Publishers, 2002; p. 74.

"YOU HAVE MADE YOURSELF AS FAMOUS . . ." Rife, p. 174.

Chapter 11: Eureka! The Discovery of Fission

"I am sure no day will pass . . ." Rife, p. 176.

"If [the former colleague] asks . . ." Sime, p. 212.

"Can you seriously think that anyone . . ." Sime, p. 212.

"I had regarded this work . . ." Sime, p. 213.

"Perhaps you cannot fully appreciate . . ." Hamilton, p. 77.

"I often feel like a wound-up . . ." Rife, p. 180.

"On all very difficult questions . . ." McGrayne, p. 52.

"It is now practically eleven . . ." Rife, p. 183.

"Perhaps you can suggest . . ." Rhodes, p. 253.

"Your radium results are very amazing . . ." Rhodes, p. 253.

"We cannot hush up the results . . ." Rhodes, p. 254.

"From these experiments, we must . . ." Rife, p. 187.

"Perhaps it is all wrong . . ." McGrayne, p. 58.

"Perhaps a drop could divide . . ." Rife, p. 189.

"The charge of a uranium nucleus . . ." Rife, pp. 189–90.

"Here was the source of all that energy . . ." Rife, p. 190.

Chapter 12: Chain Reaction

"[Frisch and I] have read your work . . ." Rhodes, p. 261.

"You are in a much better position . . ." McGrayne, pp. 59–60.

"Believe me, although I stand here . . ." McGrayne, p. 60.

"For me the uranium work . . ." McGrayne, p. 60.

"I had hardly begun to tell him . . ." Rhodes, p. 261.

"Currently planning various new experiments . . ." Rife, p. 205.

"I was immediately frightened . . ." Rife, pp. 210–11.

"I need not say how extremely delighted . . ." Rife, pp. 208–9.

"Last week the Hahn report . . ." Rife, p. 209.

"Work [of] the three of us . . ." Rife, p. 212.

"Owed nothing to physics!" Rife, p. 213.

"You and Strassmann," Rife, p. 214.

"Oh, what dumb asses . . ." McGrayne, p. 139.

"Another not very pleasant situation . . ." Sime, p. 272.

"One can imagine that when heavy nuclei . . ." Rife, p. 142.

"The gentlemen Otto Hahn and Fritz Strassmann . . ." Sime, p. 272.

"Nothing could better illustrate . . ." Sime, p. 272.

"I personally feel that these things . . ." Rife, p. 217.

"No," Pflaum, *Grand Obsession*, p. 342.

"If *we* persisted in *not* publishing . . ." Rife, pp. 223–24.

"I never thought of that!" Rife, p. 225.

"August 2, 1939, Sir . . ." Rife, pp. 225–26.

"My dear Professor . . ." Rife, p. 226.

Chapter 13: War

"To find a way to make . . ." Emling, p. 177.

"Zip," Rife, p. 234.

"I became a Communist because . . ." McGrayne, p. 140.

"A sacrifice for the feminist cause . . ." McGrayne, p. 137.

"I am not one of those . . ." McGrayne, p. 137.

"I will have nothing to do . . ." Sime, p. 305.

"Dear Otto, I am writing in a great hurry . . ." Rife, pp. 249–50.

"It is an unfortunate accident that . . ." McGrayne, p. 61.

"Women have a great responsibility . . ." Rife, p. 253.

"As long as Professor Meitner was in Germany . . ." McGrayne, p. 61.

"It grieves us that a great country like the USA . . ." Dry, pp. 146–47.

"The immense reserves of energy contained . . ." Emling, p. 187.

Chapter 14: Overlooked

"For his discovery of the fission . . ." Nobelprize.org. Nobel Media AB 2014. Web. 25 Nov 2014. <http://nobelprize.org/nobel_prizes/chemistry/laureates/1944/press.html>

"What does it matter that Lise Meitner . . ." McGrayne, p. 56.

"Long before the release of nuclear energy . . ." Sime, pp. 326–27.

"Surely Hahn fully deserved the Nobel Prize . . ." Sime, p. 327.

"In 1944, it was not officially known . . ." McGrayne, p. 61.

"I regard it as a fairness." Sime, p. 329.

"A Jewess Found the Clue," Sime, p. 323.

"Never touched upon physics . . ." Sime, p. 324.

"How can Germany regain . . ." Sime, p. 335.

"I do not think [the German people] . . ." McGrayne, p. 61.

"Suppresses the past with all his might . . ." Sime, p. 345.

"When I heard a very objective report . . ." Rife, p. xv.

"Like it or not . . ." Sime, p. 340.

"This discovery of fission . . ." Nobelprize.org. Nobel Media AB 2014. Web. 25 Nov 2014. <http://nobelprize.org/nobel_prizes/chemistry/laureates/1944/press.html>

"The energy of nuclear physical reactions . . ." "Otto Hahn—Nobel Lecture: From the Natural Transmutations of Uranium to its Artificial Fission." Nobelprize.org. Nobel Media AB 2014. Web. 25 Nov 2014. <http://www.nobelprize.org/nobel_prizes/chemistry/laureates/1944/hahn-lecture.html>

"I found it quite painful . . ." Sime, p. 344.

"Was as convinced as I am that this would be the best . . ." Sime, p. 353.

"I personally believe that I cannot live . . ." Sime, pp. 353–54.

Chapter 15: Afterward: Physicists, Pacifists, Realists

"Well, at least they are consistent . . ." Pflaum, *Grand Obsession*, p. 421.

"I am not surprised to have been arrested . . ." McGrayne, p. 142.

"I am not afraid of death . . ." McGrayne, p. 142.

"I have had some very hard moments . . ." Pflaum, *Grand Obsession*, p. 464.

"Our occupational disease," McGrayne, p. 143.

"So you're the little lady . . ." Rife, p. xv.

"I do not see why everybody is making such a fuss . . ." Rife, p. 256.

"You would be one of the best . . ." Sime, p. 350.

"Not political or anti-Semitic . . ." Sime, p. 350.

"I knew very little about the details . . ." Sime, p. 350.

"The motives of personal relationships . . ." Sime, pp. 350–51.

"Be quiet, Hahnchen . . ." McGrayne, p. 49.

"Keep your back straight . . ." McGrayne, p. 49.

BIBLIOGRAPHY

Cornwell, John. *Hitler's Scientists: Science, War, and the Devil's Pact.* New York: Viking, 2003.

Curie, Eve. *Madame Curie: A Biography.* Translated by Vincent Sheean. New York: Doubleday, 1937; reprint, Da Capo Press, 2001.

Des Jardins, Julie. *The Madame Curie Complex: The Hidden History of Women in Science.* New York: The Feminist Press at CUNY, 2010.

Dry, Sarah. *Curie.* London: Haus Publishing, 2003.

Emling, Shelley. *Marie Curie and Her Daughters: The Private Lives of Science's First Family.* New York: Palgrave Macmillan, 2012.

Frisch, Otto. "Lise Meitner, 1878–1968." *Biographical Memoirs of Fellows of the Royal Society* 16 (1970): 405–26.

Hamilton, Janet. *Lise Meitner: Pioneer of Nuclear Fission:* Berkeley Heights, NJ: Enslow Publishers, 2002.

Kiernan, Denise. *The Girls of Atomic City: The Untold Story of the Women Who Helped Win World War II.* New York: Touchstone, 2013.

McGrayne, Sharon Bertsch. *Nobel Prize Women in Science: Their Lives, Struggles and Momentous Discoveries.* Washington, D.C.: Joseph Henry Press, 1993.

Meitner, L., and O. Frisch. "Disintegration of Uranium by Neutrons: A New Type of Nuclear Reaction." *Nature* 143 (1939): 239.

Pflaum, Rosalynd. *Grand Obsession: Madame Curie and Her World.* New York: Doubleday, 1989.

Pflaum, Rosalynd. *Marie Curie and Her Daughter Irène.* Minneapolis: Lerner Publications, 1993.

Preston, Diana. *Before the Fallout: From Marie Curie to Hiroshima.* New York: Berkley Books, 2005.

Quinn, Susan. *Marie Curie: A Life.* Da Capo Press, 1995.

Redniss, Lauren. *Radioactive: Marie & Pierre Curie: A Tale of Love and Fallout.* New York: It Books, 2011.

Reid, Robert. *Marie Curie.* New York: Saturday Review Press, 1974.

Rhodes, Richard. *The Making of the Atomic Bomb: The 25th Anniversary Edition.* New York: Simon & Schuster, 2012.

Rife, Patricia. *Lise Meitner and the Dawn of the Nuclear Age.* Boston: Birkhauser, 1999, 2007.

Sime, Ruth Lewin. *Lise Meitner: A Life in Physics.* Berkeley, California: University of California Press, 1996.

Vare, Ethlie Ann, and Greg Ptacek. *Mothers of Invention: From the Bra to the Bomb, Forgotten Women and their Unforgettable Ideas.* New York: Quill, 1987.

Weston, Tom. *Fission: Based on a True Story.* Boston: Tom Weston Media, 2011.

FOR MORE INFORMATION

About the Atomic Bomb

Bagott, Jim. *The First War of Physics: The Secret History of the Atomic Bomb, 1939–1949*. New York: Pegasus, 2011.

Bird, Kai, and Martin Sherwin. *American Prometheus: The Triumph and Tragedy of J. Robert Oppenheimer*, New York: Vintage Books, 2006.

Fetter-Vorm, Jonathan. *Trinity: A Graphic History of the First Atomic Bomb*. New York: Hill and Wang, 2013.

Kelly, Cynthia C. and Richard Rhodes. *The Manhattan Project: The Birth of the Atomic Bomb in the Words of Its Creators, Eyewitnesses, and Historians*. New York: Black Dog and Leventhal Publishers, 2009.

Sheinkin, Steve. Bomb: *The Race to Build—and Steal—the World's Most Dangerous Weapon*. New York: Flash Point, 2012.

Walker, J. Samuel. *Prompt and Utter Destruction: Truman and the Use of the Atomic Bombs against Japan,* revised edition. Chapel Hill, NC: University of North Carolina Press, 2005.

About Fission

Jaffe, Bernard. Crucibles: *The Story of Chemistry from Ancient Alchemy to Nuclear Fission*. New York: Dover, 1976.

Mahaffey, James. *Nuclear Fission Reactors*. New York: Facts on File, 2011.

Whiting, Jim. *Otto Hahn and the Story of Nuclear Fission*. Hockessin, DE: Mitchell Lane Publishers, 2003.

About Radioactivity

Goldsmith, Barbara. *Obsessive Genius: The Inner World of Marie Curie*. New York: W. W. Norton, 2005.

Henderson, Harry. *The Curie Family: Exploring Radioactivity*. New York: Chelsea House, 2012.

Jerome, Kate Boehm. *Science Quest: Atomic Universe: The Quest to Discover Radioactivity*. Washington, DC: National Geographic Children's Books, 2006.

Malley, Marjorie. *Radioactivity: A History of a Mysterious Science*. London: Oxford University Press, 2011.

Nelson, Craig. *The Age of Radiance: The Epic Rise and Dramatic Fall of the Atomic Era*. New York: Scribner, 2014.

Pasachoff, Naomi. *Marie Curie: And the Science of Radioactivity*. London: Oxford University Press, 1997.

WEB RESOURCES

....

www.aip.org
American Institute of Physics; includes photos, oral histories, and biographies of leading physicists, as well as information about the institute.

www.aps.org
American Physical Society; includes biographies, history, and current events in the world of physics, as well as information about the society.

www.atomicarchive.com
Atomic Archive; includes photographs, biographies, and the history of the atomic bomb.

www.atomicheritage.org
Atomic Heritage; includes oral histories, biographies, and other information about the Manhattan Project.

www.chemheritage.org
Chemical Heritage Foundation; a searchable database with information about chemistry and chemists.

www.chemistryexplained.com
Chemistry Explained; a searchable database of encyclopedia-entry articles about chemists and chemistry.

www.famousfemalescientists.com
Famous Female Scientists; includes profiles of leading women in astronomy, biology, chemistry, and physics.

www.humantouchofchemistry.com
Human Touch of Chemistry; a website for children that explains the basics of chemistry and profiles leading scientists.

www.nobelprize.org
The official site of the Nobel Prize; includes photos, biographical information, speeches, and a searchable database.

www.nuclearmuseum.org
National Museum of Nuclear Science and History; the website of the museum, located in Albuquerque, New Mexico.

ACKNOWLEDGMENTS

For their magic in turning a manuscript into a book, I thank the team at Algonquin Young Readers: Sarah Alpert, Emma Boyer, Steve Godwin, Brunson Hoole, Elise Howard, Trevor Ingerson, Eileen Lawrence, Kelly Clark Policelli, Laura Williams, and Anne Winslow.

For her assistance and patience tracking down photographs, I thank Massiot Anais, archivist at the Curie Museum in Paris, France.

For her support of my career, I thank my agent, Sarah Davies, Greenhouse Literary Agency.

For their ongoing support of me as a writer, I thank my critique group: Erin Barker, Tami Lewis Brown, Jess Leader, Jan Lower, Lori Steel, and Helen Zax.

For their patience with me when I got lost inside this project, I thank my family: Jonathan, Hannah, Ella, and Gwendolyn.

INDEX

Page numbers in italics refer to photos and their captions.